CN01647839

BEYOND THE DRAGON PROW

On the eve of his son's birth, the Viking leader Sven Fork-Beard heard a devastating prophecy: the child would be "a cripple among cripples", he would "go through death and beyond", and worst of all, he would bring his father's line to an end.

The birth of Stiglaf was not a happy occasion. His beautiful and gentle mother, whom Sven Fork-Beard had brought to the North from the Islands to the West had died in childbirth, and the child himself was indeed a cripple. The prophecy had begun to unfold.

Instead of learning the ways of warriors, as the other children did, Stiglaf grew up learning tolerance and understanding for other people. He wandered into the mountains to befriend the strange nomadic reindeer people, and his own people shook their heads in dismay: could this be the child of Sven Fork-Beard, their great leader?

Finally cast out from the harsh world of the Vikings, Stiglaf sailed towards unknown lands and the fulfilment of the prophecy.

This Viking adventure, based on sound historical knowledge, is also a parable about friendship and humanity. It questions the hard Viking ideals of physical strength and heroism in battle, and in its hero, Stiglaf, offers for contrast many more modern virtues, including that of tolerance.

Beyond the Dragon Prow

ROBERT LEESON

COLLINS
St James's Place London

William Collins Sons & Co Ltd
London · Glasgow · Sydney . Auckland
Toronto · Johannesburg

First published 1973
© Robert A. Leeson

ISBN 0 00 184061 4

Made and Printed in Great Britain by
William Collins Sons & Co Ltd Glasgow

For Christine and Fred

This story is about Vikings, or "Northmen" as the people from Norway called themselves over 1,000 years ago, and still do today.

The Skallings are an imaginary people, living by one of the Northern fjords. For them the British Isles would be the islands "to the West". The "southern sea" is the Mediterranean, "Serkland the Great" is the Arab kingdoms and "Narvesund" the Straits of Gibraltar.

Harald Fine-Hair, king of Norway, did live, and in his time Viking ships did raid as far as the Mediterranean, and it is said they came back with "black prisoners". One Arab scribe recalled that a slave was forced to board a blazing ship with her dead Viking chieftain.

For the rest of my story, I will tell you two proverbs of the "Northmen".

"Never be first to break a friendship. Sorrow eats the heart if you cannot speak all that is in you."

"A lame man can go on horseback, a man without hands can herd cattle, a deaf man can fight and win. Better to be blind than to be burned. A dead man is no use to anyone."

R. L.

1

On a grey September day, Sven Fork-beard, chief of the Skallings, rode out to speak with Unna, old woman of the marshlands. He rode alone, telling no one of his journey. Twice in the evil, moss-covered bogs he lost the track, and horse and man were forced to struggle for their lives. Few but the skin-shoed nomads with their reindeer came this way, and no man came unless he had to.

Light was going from the sky when he swung down from the saddle in the shadow of a huge rock. Sven was tall and powerful; his hair, coarse and black as his horse's mane, glistened in the autumn drizzle. His black cloak was held at the throat by a silver brooch that gleamed in the eerie greyness. Turning, he scanned each bush and stunted clump of birch and pine. Nothing moved. He shivered, shrugged his shoulders, then stepped forward and began to circle the rock. A second later he vanished from sight.

In that instant, a bush no more than a spear's throw from the rock was pushed to one side. Stooping low and moving cautiously came another man, tall like Sven, but lean, with tawny hair and beard, his eyes restless and cunning. He was Sven's brother and men called him Red Arnulf. Soon he reached the rock and circled it as his brother had done. Soon he found what he sought, a cleft as wide as a man's body, reaching into the heart of the rock. Bracing himself, he pushed his way in. For a moment he seemed in pitch darkness, but ahead was a wavering light. The passage curved and Arnulf was suddenly at the mouth of a cave, full of shadows thrown by fire that leapt and crackled in the centre. Silhouetted against the flames stood his brother, peering into the blackness beyond. Both men, watcher and watched, waited, hardly breathing.

There was a movement in the darkness, something thrown on the fire, and a sudden greenish blaze lit up Sven's black hair and powerful features. From the dark emptiness came an old woman's soft chuckle. Arnulf shivered and drew back into the cleft as if he had been seen. The old voice spoke.

"Unna sees Sven Fork-beard, chief among the Skallings. He has ridden far, ridden where few men go and fewer return. His need must be great."

The black-haired giant shook himself and answered:

"My need is great. The need of the Skallings is great. I must know . . ."

Another chuckle, more high-pitched, interrupted him.

"I know what you must know. I know that for twenty years you have led the Skallings in peace and war, more often in war, for this is the way of the Skallings. And I know that your brother, Arnulf the Red, has fought beside you all these years. Between you, you have made the Skallings mighty and feared – to the islands of the west, to the south where seas are warm. You have sailed west and south and have come back with death and plunder.

"And I know that two winters ago you brought back a woman from the islands of the west and made her your wife, which did not please the old men. And since then she has taught you to turn away from war and raiding and get your wealth from the rich soil of the Skalling valley. And that has not pleased the young men.

"And now you are to have a child. But such is the way of things, Arnulf your brother, too, will have a child. And you must know which will be born first, to make sure that your son will one day lead the Skallings and not the son of Red Arnulf. If, that is, the child be a boy. Oh, yes, Sven Fork-beard, there is much you would know of Unna, perhaps more than a man should know."

Sven cleared his throat and his voice burst out. "These things will answer themselves and soon. Within days my child and Arnulf's will be born. But I must know more – and I have brought gifts . . ."

"Ha! I will tell you what it pleases me to tell you. You might give me all the gold you have gathered from the coasts around the western and southern seas, and I might tell you nothing. What more must you know?"

Sven answered: "I must know. Will my son be true to my ways? Will he lead the Skallings in peace?"

Again the soft chuckling came from the darkness. "Will he be true to the ways his mother has taught you, ways that may not please the Skallings? What sort of an answer do you need?"

"I must know the truth. I must be sure. Tell me all."

There was a long silence, only broken by the crackle from the flames as the fire burned lower. Then Unna spoke again:

"Sven Fork-beard. There is no man living who does not wish to know all, but few to whom it is granted. There is no man to whom it is granted who does not wish he had known nothing. But I will tell you all if you must know it."

"I must."

Now the fire burned up again and the cave began to fill with heavy smoke, so that Arnulf was forced to draw back farther into the cleft and thrust his fist into his mouth to prevent a cough from betraying him. But he dared not go too far from the fire, for the voice began again, this time low and dream-like.

"Sven Fork-beard, hear me closely. You will have a son and he will be born before you return to your home. His coming will bring you joy and great sorrow."

The voice fell silent and Sven cried out: "More, tell more."

"Your son will be a true son of his father . . . will you hear more?"

"Tell me all."

"Your son will never bear sword and will never rule the Skallings."

The great man by the fire shuddered. In the shadows of the cleft his brother's brown eyes glittered.

"Your son will be a cripple among cripples.

"Your son will go through death and beyond.

"Your son will be called Stiglaf and he will bring your line to an end."

A shout of anger and pain came from the black-haired chief.

"No, that cannot be. That cannot be all."

And from the dark beyond the flames came the answer: "That is all."

His face twisted with anger and shame, Sven Fork-beard rushed from the firelight and the cave, passing so close in the cleft entrance that he almost touched the man hiding there. In another second he was gone, blundering down the

narrow chasm and out into the pale sky of the marshlands. Sven's brother turned too and was about to creep away down the narrow passage when the old woman spoke again.

"Wait, Red Arnulf, wait. You have hidden and spied on your brother, at risk of your life. Do you want to know what awaits you? Or have you heard enough? Does the misfortune of your brother satisfy you, or do you wish to hear what I can tell of your fate?"

The man gasped and swallowed painfully. His voice came out thin and hard.

"I have no gifts, old Unna."

"Gifts? What are they? I will tell you freely what the coming time and the time beyond will bring you. If you truly will know."

"Yes," breathed Arnulf, "I will know."

"Then hear me, Arnulf the Red. You will have a son and he will be born before you return to your home. His coming will bring you joy.

"Your son will be red and a warrior, as bold and cruel as you.

"Your son will rule over the Skallings, for Stiglaf, son of Sven, is fated to follow you on the longest voyage.

"Your son shall take death to the southern seas and carry it back.

"Your son will be called Torald and at his death he will be lower than the lowest."

"But, why . . . what . . . ?" gabbled Arnulf.

"Ask no more questions. I have told you all. Now you must go back to your home and live out your life – what remains of it."

These last words sank into the depths of Arnulf's mind, as the flames died away to embers. As he stumbled down the cleft out into the grey twilight and picked his way across the marshes to his waiting horse, he had already begun to put them from his mind. As he urged his horse, slipping and stumbling down the mountain trails, he fixed his mind on keeping to the track and keeping at a safe distance from the huge black figure of Sven farther down the trail.

When the two brothers drew near their home valley, Arnulf swung his horse away from the trail and circled the edge of the hills that lay around, so that he would enter the stronghold of the Skallings from a different direction. Sven must never know that he, Arnulf, knew the secrets of both of them – all that his brother knew and more.

As the two brothers rode into the valley from either end,

fires burned and lights flickered round their homes. The women had gathered for the birth of two sons.

In Arnulf's home there was joy for a son, red like his father.

In Sven's home there was joy and sorrow. As the child was born, his mother, the woman from the islands of the west, was dying.

The oldest and most skilful woman, who acted as midwife, looked keenly into smokey light of torches and fire at the newly-born boy.

"Fair, like his mother," she said, shaking her head. Then she noticed another thing, and, snatching up the child, she wrapped it carefully in soft hide and took it away into a darkened back room.

2

As the long winter nights came down on the valley of the Skallings, Sven Fork-beard stayed in his home and brooded. For the third year no ships had sailed for the southern and western waters. The younger men muttered among themselves but did not dare to raise their voices in the fire hall. Sven was so savage in his grief after the loss of his fair-haired wife that he could not bear even to look at his new-born son. The older men and his closest companions – Jofur, his singer and spokesman, Eynor, his right-hand man and spear-carrier – knew that they must wait for Sven's mood to change. They suspected that there was a deeper grief and did not dare to ask.

Arnulf the Red, whom the young men looked to as their leader, disappointed them by keeping his peace. He went further, and warned them to be patient and wait, for the future would bring changes. Even when winter came to an end and the first red rim of the returning sun showed over the edge of the landward mountains, and Sven still gave no order for the longships to be made ready, Arnulf made no protest.

With the spring and the warmer, longer days, Sven suddenly came from his home and began to give orders for the cattle to be driven to the mountain pastures. He set the young men to clearing fresh parts of the valley woods and levelling the ground for crops. As the days grew still longer, he appeared to take note of the grumbling of the younger men and set Eynor to train and exercise the youngest of them – those who had been boys only the year before – in the use of sword and spear, or to take their place at the long-ship oars. But still there was not talk of a voyage.

One fine May day, Jofur the skald, the only man in the valley apart from Arnulf and Eynor who dared to speak to Sven's face while his black mood lasted, found the chief by the edge of the water, looking down the fjord.

"Will you sail again, Sven Fork-beard?" he asked.

Sven shook his great black head.

"No, not this year, nor the next," he said.

"But why do you have Eynor train the young boys?"

"Because it is the custom and they grow restless."

"But they will be grown men without knowing battle or the far seas."

"Yes, they will live long, and live to thank me for that."

"But our people grow in numbers. Your child and Red Arnulf's were not the only ones to be born last year. One day there will not be room enough."

"Then we must make room, clear the forests and till the soil."

"But . . ."

"No more, Jofur. If you want songs to sing, then sing of old battles. Those songs are best and living men can hear them."

Summer came and went. The weather was good. The harvest, both from the land and the sea, was rich. It needed every hand, man, woman, boy and girl, to carry it in. The grain stores were full, great stocks of fish were dried. The women wove and stitched new clothing and sang. For three years no man had died in the valley except in his sleeping-place. The women gossiped too, about the new children in the valley, about Torald, red like his father Arnulf, and as fierce, it was said, and about Stiglaf, son of Sven, who was as fair and golden as his mother and whom no one but the women in Sven's house had seen at close hand. That was strange, they said. And it was whispered that Stiglaf was hidden away because Sven was angry over the death of the boy's mother. But no one knew the truth.

When the autumn and the dark days came again and the sun vanished behind the mountains, when storms tore the sea beyond the rocky headlands at the mouth of the fjord, Sven appeared again in the fire hall. Warriors, young and old, gathered on the benches, and Jofur, Sven's skald, and Sigurd, singer and spokesman for Arnulf, sang in turn of battles in far-off lands, of expeditions to the islands of the west and to the edge of the southern seas. As the drinking vessels were passed around, excitement grew until one young man spoke up.

"Sven Fork-beard, say to us. Shall we see such battles again, or must we all learn women's ways?"

Sven answered mildly, "You are young and healthy and know battles only in song. When our fathers, long ago, settled in this valley, they knew how to dig the soil and fight for what they had when they needed to. There was no talk of women's ways."

There was silence for a while, then another young man, who had sailed more than once in Arnulf's ship, spoke up:

"That is true. How can a boy who has seen no battle know what are men's and what are women's ways? But there are those among us who want to feel the ship riding beneath us again over the waves and see the dragon prow point to the west and south."

There was a murmur of agreement, though the older men saw Sven's frown and shook their heads. The young warrior, growing bolder, spoke again:

"Tell us, Sven Fork-beard. Every man here knows you are a great leader of the Skallings. In all the fjords to the south and north, there is none greater. But men say that you have pledged yourself never to sail forth again and that you will bring up your son in the same manner, that the Skallings will have a farmer for a leader, not a warrior."

At this there was a rumbling from the benches where the men of Sven's ship sat and some of the older men called out, "Peace, let the skald sing again."

But Sven's voice, harsh with anger, sounded over the noise:

"When his time comes, my son will be worthy of his father."

From the darkness of the farthest corner of the hall, behind the benches where Arnulf's ship-men sat and drank, someone called.

"No one doubts it, but we have not seen him yet. Only the women have seen him. We have seen Torald, son of Arnulf, crawl and play at his father's door, but we have never seen Stiglaf, son of Sven."

The row between the benches became deafening. Hands flew to sword hilts, seats were overturned, and in the midst of it all, Arnulf stood up in the open space before the fire and quietened the noise with a sweep of his hand. He turned to Sven and said calmly:

"Brother, the two boys are now one year old. Both can stand and look about them. Let them be brought into the

hall so that our comrades may see them, just as we two were brought in the days of our father."

Sven's face was stone hard. He stared into the fire a moment, then, shrugging, he called to Eynor. "Let the women bring in the boys."

There was a moment's quiet and then Torald's mother came through the doorway with the red-haired child, half-awake in her arms. At a sign from Arnulf, she took aside the wrappings and set the boy down on his feet in the centre of the hall. As the boy's opened eyes caught sight of his father, he began to march with comic waddling step towards him. The young men from Arnulf's crew began to chant:

"Heya, Torald, Torald the Red," as the father swung up his son and placed him back in his mother's arms.

Now the old woman who carried Stiglaf appeared in the firelit circle. She pulled away the clothes around him and the men saw for the first time how fair and yellow his hair was and how black was that of his father. The old woman moved to hand the child to his father, where he sat in the midst of his ship-men, but Arnulf said:

"Put the lad down. Let him find his own way to his father."

The old woman hesitated. Sven nodded grimly and she lowered Stiglaf to the rough log floor. Then the men nearest to the boy nudged one another and pointed. One foot was perfectly formed, but the other was shortened and twisted. When the child tried to move forward the deformed foot crumpled over and he tottered forward on to his face with a cry.

A drunken voice from beyond the firelight shouted:

"Heya, Stiglaf the Unsteady."

There was a burst of laughter from the benches around Arnulf – a tense silence from the other side of the hall. Eynor leapt forward, caught up the child and swung it to his leather-clad shoulder. Drawing his sword he stood out into the space between the benches and shouted again and again until Sven's warriors joined in chorus:

"Heya, Stiglaf, son of Sven!"

3

The valley had three rich summers, one after another. The sea leapt with fish and the hill-slopes shone with corn. The Skalling people had so much that they traded dried meat for fox furs with the people to the north. But there was no sailing out. The longboats were beached and scoured and the seams caulked and the young boys were trained by Eynor – racing and wrestling and swimming the width of the inlet at its narrow point within sight of the fire hall.

Torald, now called the Red, after his father, amazed young and old by his strength, leaping into the water like a seal, when he could barely stagger on land, hurling stones as far as older boys and fighting anyone, boy or dog, that passed his path, his face as red and furious as the colour of his hair. Arnulf, his father, amiable and joking, directed the young men as they worked over his longship, turning aside their grumbles and demands when they grew impatient to go on long voyages.

Stiglaf, called son of Sven in the hearing of the older men, and at other times Stiglaf the Unsteady, did not run, nor did he swim, for his trailing leg made him fear the water. A craftsman made him a small shoe of leather bound to a well-shaped sole of wood and the clack clack of his foot on the stones signalled his unsteady approach.

Sven directed his ship-men in the care of their longboat and the people of the valley in their work with the crops and herds. In his black beard glistened streaks of silver, like the silver of the brooch he wore at his throat, the brooch given him long ago by Stiglaf's mother. With Sven there was no joking, and since the autumn night when the two boys were shown to the men, no one questioned him about voyages. He kept his grim silence and no one challenged it. And for six years after the birth of Stiglaf and Torald, there was no sailing out.

But after the three rich years came three lean years. The fish shoals turned south and in summer the clouds hung down over the wooded slopes month after month. The sun's warmth did not reach through the mists and the green crops turned brown, not golden, and rotted away. The flanks of the cattle were rough and wrinkled and the bones showed through. For the first of the thin years the Skallings drew on their food stocks and traded no grain or meat. In the second year the stocks ran out before the winter ended. By the third year there was little left to store. But all the children born in the good years had to be fed, and the whisper "too many" was heard.

That autumn a group of young men, led by Trygve, son of Eynor, went into the woods and began to cut timber. In the spring, instead of joining in the work with the crops and cattle, they began to lay a keel by the inlet, some little distance from the longships of Sven and Arnulf. As their ship took shape, a small, sturdy vessel with sixteen oars, the people in the valley waited to know what Sven would say. But no meet was called. It was as though young and old alike were pretending that what was happening was not happening.

One day, at dawn, when the ship was nearly ready, Trygve stood by the shore alone. Suddenly he saw that Sven stood by him.

"Trygve? Why are you taking away the young men?" the black-bearded chief asked.

"Sven Fork-beard," replied the young man. "What shall we do? There are enough hands to bring in the crops, such as they will be, and to haul in the fish if there will be any. We are not needed."

Sven shook his head. "If the harvest is heavy, we shall need every hand. Dead men cannot till the land."

"Nor do they need food," replied Trygve shortly, and turned his back to walk away, half expecting a blaze of anger from Sven. But none came. The leader stood silent by the shore as Trygve marched up the slope towards his home. After several days the young man and his companions, harnessed and armed, went down to their ship and climbed aboard. They took few provisions, for there was little enough to eat in the valley for the people they left behind.

Silently the Skallings crowded the shore to watch them go. Sven climbed up to the rocky point and remained there long after the young men's oars had carried their ship down the fjord and round the headland. He stayed there looking out to sea even after the families of the young men had gone back to their own homes.

In the evening, and on days that followed, the old men talked about the voyage of the young men and shook their heads over what might happen to them without the skilled leadership and guidance of men like Sven, Arnulf and Eynor to guide them. The young men talked too, but of the exploits they imagined Trygve and his ship-men performing, of the landfalls they would be making, the bold raids and cunning retreats, the spoils they would take. But as the year wore on the time came when all that could be said had been spoken and no one talked any more of Trygve and his crew. Not because they were forgotten, but because talking could not bring them back and could only bring pain to their families. That summer was harder than the three before it. Even the hay would not dry on the hurdles. Before the first berries ripened there was real hunger in the valley, and Sven sent the children and even some of the young men to hunt the small animals that crept through the woods for food. When evening came and people drew together on the open slope above the shoreline in the misty half-light, the talk was of food, of past good harvests, and years when the fish came leaping up the fjord, so thick that a man might walk on their backs – or so it was said. Every day someone, man, woman or child, would climb to the top of the rocky point that jutted out to the seaward side of the settlement and look down the fjord and over the headland to the sea beyond. It might be that they would see the small ship with the sixteen young men returning. This was done every day as the months passed, even when no one spoke of Trygve's crew any more, but only of food and past harvests. As autumn came even the young men's families began to lose hope, and only the most faithful would make the climb to the top of the rock. But there was one young girl who never failed to go each day and sit for an hour or more in the cool, damp air, staring into the grey distance, hoping always to see a dot on the horizon, a tiny square sail, the dim silhouette of a dragon prow.

One afternoon before the light faded, when a misty rain was falling and young and old had crept indoors to eat silently the one slender meal of the day, this girl stayed on the rock, ignoring the rain that soaked into her clothes, peering half-blinded into the haze. The people living nearest to the shore heard her scream again and again as she scrambled and fell and ran from her lookout point.

"Ships, ships, ships!"

In minutes the homes were empty, hunger was forgotten. Excitement drove the Skallings in a great crowd to the shore. The youngest raced to clamber up the rock and strain their eyes into the greyness between sea and sky.

"Ships, many ships!" came the cry.

Soon others reached the top of the rock, among them a man older than all the rest. His eyes, still keen, took in the dozens of black points that rose and fell on the far edge of the sea.

They were not ships.

"Whales, whales!" he shrieked, and seized the black cloak of Sven who had just reached the head of the rock. "Whales. They never came so close since I was a boy."

Sven's grave face softened and the people near him saw something they had not seen for years. Sven smiled. He turned and sent out a great shout that echoed to the wooded hills beyond the homesteads.

"Launch the boats."

For ten days the whales swam off the headland and for ten days the hungry Skallings desperately slaughtered them, lugging the carcasses to shore where the women and children flayed and hacked the huge mammals' flesh till the shore flooded black with blood and the air reeked. Again and again the boats set out and returned with their snorting, threshing victims. The whales were dying, but the Skallings would live.

On the tenth day the whales, scattered by the deadly attack, were struggling out to sea. Sven made up his mind to call off the hunt. But Eynor came to him and said quietly:

"Let me take your ship and twenty of the youngest men who have never voyaged before and we will follow the whales to the south."

Sven, understanding, nodded. "Do it!" he said, and turned to direct the beaching of the last of the harpooned whales. Eynor and the youngest men, swiftly chosen, made ready, and before light faded Sven's longboat, with its black sail, slid down the fjord and made for the open sea, heading south in the track of the fleeing whales.

That night the wind changed, a storm blew up and Eynor and his crew were gone not ten days as they had planned but twice as long. On the twentieth day, the look-out on the rock spotted them again, and again the Skallings gathered. They saw the longship as it rounded the head-land, the young men heaving on the oars like seasoned sailors.

The older people anxiously began to count the oars as they rose and fell in the water. When they knew that every man was safe, they breathed more deeply.

Sven and Arnulf were the first to see that something was wrong. They hurried down to the shore just as the long-ship with her young crew drove in from the water and lodged its curving keel into the sand. There was a deep silence as Eynor clambered over the gunwale and leapt into the shadows. He carried something slung over his shoulder which he dropped down on to the sand at the feet of the two brothers. Someone in the waiting crowd gasped.

It was the harness which Trygve, Eynor's son, had worn when he and his crew of sixteen had sailed out in the spring. It was rusted, rotting and stained with sea-water. But it was Trygve's, beyond a doubt. In a few words, Eynor told how, following the whales, and then driven off course by the storm, they had decided to return and how, when still four days out from the fjord, they had crossed the great current that drifts to the north from the warmer seas. One day they found Trygve's little ship, waterlogged and sinking. Only three of her men were still on board, and they, long dead, though how they died, even Eynor's experienced eye could not tell. Had they died in battle, or of hunger and thirst, drinking the sea-water? Or, said some, had sea-creatures come up out of the depths to claim them?

Sven took Eynor by the shoulders and led him away from the beach, while the crowd followed silently, the children beginning to whimper like puppies. Sven ordered the fires to be made up in the great hall and told all but the youngest, men and women alike, to gather there. Food was made ready, the whale-meat, and when this was eaten, Sven spoke of the young men, led by Trygve, son of Eynor, and their long journey.

When he was finished, everyone sat or squatted in deep silence, while the fire threw shadows among the great rafters.

Suddenly Sigurd, the skald of Arnulf, began to sing. The older men muttered. This was not right, that Sigurd and not Jofur, Sven's skald, should sing at such a moment. But Sven raised his hand and there was quiet again.

Sigurd sang:

Our young men sailed, seeking wealth and fame
They sailed far, no one knows how far.

Courage they had, but not wisdom.
How can the young be saved, without wise men to guide them?
Without their true leaders, skilled in the ways of sea and war?
Alone on the wild waves they died, who knows how?
But we know they will not come again.

Sigurd sang on, naming each of the young men who had died, praising their families, reminding those who listened of deeds done by their families. Sven heard him out to the end, his head sunk down on his great chest.

When Stiglaf, son of Sven, grew older and was allowed to come to the fire hall, he heard the song of the lost young men many times. And he always held down his head as his father had done, so that no one should see his tears.

4

After the year of the whales there were good harvests followed by bad, but under Sven Fork-beard's careful rule, hunger was kept away. Young men, remembering the fate of Trygve and his companions, went about their work and their training with no complaint. And in these peaceful years Torald and Stiglaf grew up.

Torald fulfilled his early promise. When he was ten he stood as tall as some of the young men. When he was twelve he reached to his father's shoulder. He could swim across the fjord and back, his grip was like that of a bear, and his skill and ferocity in mock fights made the older warriors say that he would be a greater man than Arnulf. At which Red Arnulf would shrug his shoulders and laugh. "Time will show," he said. When some remarked, quietly, that Arnulf's son was better fitted to be leader of the Skallings than the son of Sven, Arnulf would frown and remind them of old custom and forbid them to talk any more of the matter. They found this strange, but Arnulf, to whom Unna had opened the door of the future, was willing to bide his time.

Sven saw everything, and as had been his habit for years since his wife had died, said little. He saw little cheer in the future as Unna had foretold it, but that could not be altered.

Now he would do what was right for the Skallings. War and the ways of war had become strange to Sven and hateful. But still he found his son Stiglaf hard to understand. Sven did not think the lad was a coward. He knew that the shortened leg and twisted foot gave him pain every day, but he made no complaint, and the pale face under the fair hair was calm, the voice quiet. Stiglaf was strong, too, in his own way. Sven had watched him help in the fields and with the cattle and saw that the awkward body had its own power and skill.

But Stiglaf refused to wear a sword, carry a spear, or to train in battle-skills, though Eynor in his rough and genial way urged him to join in. Sometimes the lad would watch the others at their training on the beach and his face would cloud at the sight of small wounds and over-eager blows.

But on most days when there was no work with cattle or crops, Stiglaf was nowhere to be seen in the valley. Holding a short staff he had cut for himself, he would limp up the slope, his shoe tapping on the rocks, and then disappear into the higher woods. There he would roam, each season going farther afield, sometimes not returning for days, sleeping on the hills among the night animals, living off berries and roots.

When Stiglaf was twelve, he found a path through the bogland and met a band of nomad people on the trail. One of them was a girl his own age. Her face was strange to him, with its high cheek bones, slanted eyes and saffron skin. The eyes were deep and dark and looked far into him. Stiglaf was cautious, for to the Skallings all nomad women, young and old, were witches. The nomads saw he was young and alone and they were friendly. The girl's brother admired the short knife that Stiglaf carried at his belt, and

Stiglaf traded it for a pair of the moccasins made from a reindeer pelt, which gripped his feet like a second skin and carried him warmly and smoothly along the forest trails. They showed him how to find the marvellous golden marsh berries which seem to come suddenly from the sky when the days are long and to vanish just as suddenly. Then the nomads vanished, just as suddenly and strangely, but smiled at him as they went.

For months afterwards the face of the girl with its slant eyes stayed in his thoughts by day and his dreams by night. He spoke to his father one evening as the chief, his black head and beard now thickly streaked with grey, sat brooding by their home fire.

"Why do the Skallings fear the people in the hills?"

Sven answered shortly: "Their ways are not ours. Their men fight from ambush and their women cast spells. Beware of the high hills, the marshland and the wanderers."

When the harvest was in and the first snows had fallen Stiglaf took dried meat in his pouch and wrapped small gifts in soft hide. He set out for the plateau to search for the nomads, but did not find them because they were farther to the east with their herds. So he pushed on where the snow was deeper, shaping himself rough round snow-shoes from thin branches tied with skin strips. After four days he had gone beyond the limit of his farthest wanderings and was caught by a sudden blizzard in the open rockland, high above the tree-line. The strain on his twisted foot was too much and he sank down to rest. He was alone in the wild wilderness. The cold outside him was stinging, biting, but inside he was warm and at peace. He fell asleep and his body slowly began to die.

The nomad girl's brother and father, circling the plateau

after lost reindeer, came upon him lying still by the trail, covered with a light powdering of snow. They brushed the snow from his face and clicked their tongues. Then swiftly they slaughtered a stray beast, ripped open its hide, removed the innards and forced his curled-up body into the reeking heat within. They carried him miles on the back of another reindeer until they caught up with the tribe in its circle of skin tents. There they gave him to the care of an old woman, who fingered his long fair hair, stripped off his clothes, and touched his twisted foot and shortened leg with her worn, dirty old hands.

Stiglaf awoke in the smokey gloom of the skin tent, his body lazy and warm. For a moment he imagined he had passed beyond life and death into the world of the wandering wind spirit.

But then in the murk of the tent he saw the face of the girl, her dark eyes smiling. And a second later he looked down at his own body and saw that his foot was no longer cramped and twisted, but he could move each toe and bend the foot. He stretched his legs and saw that one was still shorter than the other. Even the magic of the hill people could do nothing to change that. But the pain that gripped him at nights was gone and in its place was peace.

He returned to his own valley with the spring sun, wearing the skin-clothes and bright beads of the nomads, so that at first the Skalling youngsters, driving the thin cattle up to the spring pasture, did not know him. They recognised him only by his carved stick and swaying, limping walk. His father greeted him gladly, but simply, as though he knew that what would come to Stiglaf was beyond him. But Sven told his son shortly that he must put away the nomad clothes.

No one asked Stiglaf where he had been or how he had survived the winter in the marshes. But now people drew away from him, and the young men, who had been tolerant but contemptuous, eyed him with some secret fear. He was among them, but not of them.

A year passed and a new problem thrust itself at Sven and his son. Soon both Stiglaf and Torald would be old enough to be taken as men. For Torald the time had clearly come already. Though only thirteen he could match most rivals in swimming, leaping, running, and with sword or spear. But what of Stiglaf? As the months wore on Sven became more quietly perplexed and spoke discreetly with the old men. But they too were perplexed. They had never seen a lad like Stiglaf before. They said in their own minds that this was only to be expected for Sven Fork-beard had not married a woman of the Skallings but had taken one from the people of the far away western lands. Yet those thoughts they kept to themselves.

But in the summer something happened that overshadowed the problem of Stiglaf, something fateful, that touched not simply his life but the lives of all the Skallings. Stiglaf had gone into the woods some miles south of the valley, following the trail of a brown bear that had come unusually far down the hill slopes. His ears picked up a distant jingling sound, of harness – armed men on horseback. Without hesitating he reached with his long arms for the branch of a tree above him and hauled himself skilfully into the shelter of his twigs and leaves. Balanced on a bough, his back braced against the trunk, he watched the trail. There was not long to wait. The clump of horses' hooves came nearer and then, round a bend in the path, came a full score horsemen, in double file, all fully armed.

Ahead of them rode a man, also fully armed, though the plates on his leather tunic were so richly ornamented that Stiglaf gasped. When the Skalling warriors set out to war, they were well armed. Their weapons were skilfully carved with runes to protect their bearers, but he had never seen such rich decoration. Nor had he seen a face so thin, so dark, and so cruel.

When the horsemen had passed, he slithered to the ground and made his way home swiftly using secret trails. He limped breathless into his home to warn his father. Sven nodded and smiled a grim smile.

"I know these men."

And as he spoke there came from the trees the blast of a horn.

5

Outside the Skalling fire hall a score of ash-hafted spears were stacked, guarded by one of the newly-arrived horsemen who sat with harness unbuckled, drinking beer handed to him by one of the women and talking in his strange southern dialect to the young men who gathered round. Only the older Skalling men had been allowed across the threshold with the visitors.

Inside the hall, with Arnulf on one side of him and Eynor at the other, Sven sat, not in his usual place, but on a side bench so that he faced the visitors on equal ground. The man who had ridden into the valley with his twenty horsemen was feared and respected among the Northmen and mistrusted by some. His name was Cynewulf and he was an exile from the islands of the west, who had taken refuge with Harald, King of the Northmen. He had sailed on many ventures and fought in many battles among the Franks, and even as far as the southern sea. By sheer boldness, iron nerve and ruthlessness, he had made himself Harald's captain.

First Cynewulf saluted Sven and Arnulf, drinking from the horn offered him. Then Sven spoke, politely but coolly.

"Greetings, Cynewulf. What does King Harald's man want with the Skallings?"

"Greetings, Sven Fork-beard. There is no need for time-wasting. I have come to call you to join us in battle. We count on you for four-score men." He raised his hand. "It is known that the Skallings have increased in number, for it is fifteen years since the longships of Sven Fork-beard and Red Arnulf have cleared harbour. What do you say?"

Sven answered: "We will not argue over numbers. You know as does King Harald Fine-hair that if Sven Fork-beard joins battle there is no holding back, nor counting of numbers nor cost."

The Skallings murmured their agreement and Cynewulf nodded, smiling thinly. But before he could speak, Sven went on:

"But it is the custom among Northmen to know something of the cause of battle, the quarrel. Death is no stranger to us, nor has it any fear for us, but we are not cattle to be driven to slaughter without question."

Cynewulf frowned. He sensed a rebuke in Sven's tone, but allowed nothing to anger him.

Sven went on: "So what is the quarrel and where will King Harald have us sail?"

The hall was silent. Cynewulf looked down at the log floor and played with the hilt of his dagger.

"We shall sail with the King of Valland against the Princes of Serkland the Great, as far as the southern seas."

There was a rumble of excitement from the benches where the Skalling warriors sat, but Sven frowned and spoke harshly.

"Why shall we sail with the Franks? What treaties does King Harald have with the King of Valland? We know nothing of such treaties. Since when did Harald Fair-hair deal with strangers behind our backs?"

Cynewulf bit his lip. "There is no treaty. But Sven Forkbeard knows there are ties of friendship and blood-ties with Valland, where many Northmen now have strongholds. They have called for our aid in their alliance with the Franks."

"Who among the Northmen in Valland calls for our aid?"

"Gange-Rolf," answered Cynewulf.

There was a burst of amusement among the Skallings. Rolf the Walker was known far and wide. He was so huge no horse could carry him and he was obliged to walk wherever he went. But Sven's voice cut across the laughter.

"Gange-Rolf is an outlaw, driven from Viki in the south for cattle-stealing. This is no quarrel of King Harald's. What game do you play, Cynewulf? Is it for this they call you Cynewulf the Sly?"

Cynewulf gripped his dagger. The insult was clear. But again he choked back his anger and smiled craftily.

"It is many years since Gange-Rolf fled to Valland. Now he is a mighty earl among the Franks and many Northmen have joined him. Besides, Gange-Rolf is kin to King Harald and the old quarrel is forgotten."

Arnulf, choosing his moment carefully, now spoke:

"Let us hear, brother, what is the cause of battle. We have fought beside worse men than Gange-Rolf."

Cynewulf smiled his relief. "The Franks are hard-pressed by the princes of Serkland the Great. If the Franks yield to them, who knows where they will stop? Already they hold all the land from the Black Sea to Narvesund, the narrow straits of the southern sea."

Sven raised his hand:

"Why cannot the Franks treat with their enemies? They

are rich. They have bought and sold armies and kingdoms before now."

Cynewulf replied slowly: "This is no ordinary war. This is a war that can be ended only with victory. This is a war over the gods and men's belief in them. One may not give way to the other. Right is right and wrong is wrong."

In the silence that followed one of the oldest men suddenly spoke up: "Gods, what gods? I have heard . . ." he turned chuckling to the crowd on the Skalling benches. "I have heard that the Franks say there is only one god, wherever men walk and beasts run. And I was told, long ago, that the princes of Serkland hold that there is only one god. So," said the old man triumphantly, "where is the quarrel?"

Cynewulf joined in the sudden burst of laughter that came from both sides. "Old man," said he. "Each will have it that the one god is their own."

"I have heard," the old man persisted, "that Harald Fair-hair's house has many who say the Frankish god is the one true god. Is it for this, which means nothing to Skallings, that our warriors shall sail south?" The old man climbed from his bench and paced about the log floor. "They say that this god is called the Prince of Peace. Why does he want to make war?"

"Even a prince of peace must make himself secure against attack," replied Cynewulf, whose followers and many of the Skallings nodded their heads and tapped their feet at the shrewdness of his answer.

Arnulf rose: "I have no care for the one god of the Franks, nor for anyone else's one god. We Skallings pray each in his own home. But tell me, Cynewulf, captain of Harald Fine-hair, will there be honour for our young men in this war and will they bring riches home to our valley with the victory?"

"As much of both as they can bear," replied Cynewulf, and a mutter of approval swelled among the younger men to a shouting and stamping of feet. Sven spoke:

"Cynewulf, Harald's captain. You have spoken openly. We shall be as true with you. But these things must be decided among the Skallings. You are welcome to stay with us seven days and enjoy the best we have to offer you. Before you ride south again, you shall have a straight answer."

With that the meet ended and three days of feasting followed. Cynewulf's men tried their strength against the Skalling warriors in all the sports and war skills. There was excitement and cheer in the valley such as had not been seen for many years. Only the oldest men and some of the women, it seemed, brooded over the future and what it might bring. And Sven Fork-beard. He would pace up and down inside his own home fingering the brooch his wife had given him. Or he would walk the shore-line at dusk, his great head jutting forward like a charging bull. After five days' deep thought, he quietly called together Arnulf, Eynor, the ablest of the warriors and the most experienced of the old men. One by one he asked them to speak. All but two of the old men told him that the Skallings should send their four-score warriors to fight alongside the Franks.

Sven nodded: "I will not speak against it, though in my heart I do not like it."

"But who will lead them, Sven Fork-beard?" asked Eynor. "Once before, young men sailed away and where are they now?"

Arnulf looked straight at Sven. "With four-score men we

must send both longships. I am ready to captain my ship, and my son Torald will sail with me."

Sven's eyes gleamed. The challenge in Arnulf's words was clear. The air was tense with unspoken insult and Eynor intervened.

"Sven Fork-beard's heart is turned against war. It is not for fear. No man dare say that. But his heart is turned against war and I will captain his ship. If my son were alive, he would sail with me."

"And who will sail from Sven's house?" asked Sigurd, Arnulf's skald. "Shall Stiglaf, son of Sven, sail?"

Someone laughed, then quickly clapped a hand to his mouth. No one spoke. Men shifted uneasily.

"No," said Sven in a voice like thunder. "Stiglaf shall not sail, will not sail. But Sven shall captain his own ship."

6

In a month, the four-score warriors were chosen and the two longboats made ready. The excitement which had risen over Cynewulf's visit and the news that Sven Fork-beard would sail at the head of the band, now died down. There was enough for everyone to do. Harvest-time was coming and the work of bringing in the crops would be doubled for those who remained. From every homestead a young warrior had been picked. Among them were ten who had never sailed before, and chief among these was Torald, so tall now that he looked like a brother to Arnulf, not a son.

Stiglaf, who had always walked alone, discovered that now he could feel even more lonely. He knew that if he had not been a cripple his father would not have made this voyage – breaking the secret pledge he had made to Stiglaf's mother. But when he sat in the evening with his father, he could see no reproach in the black-bearded face, only sadness. When the day came for leaving, Stiglaf went to Sven.

"Father, take me with you."

But Sven shook his head and gripped Stiglaf by the shoulder. "You are my true son and you must live, for there are things still to do. I know that you are no coward,

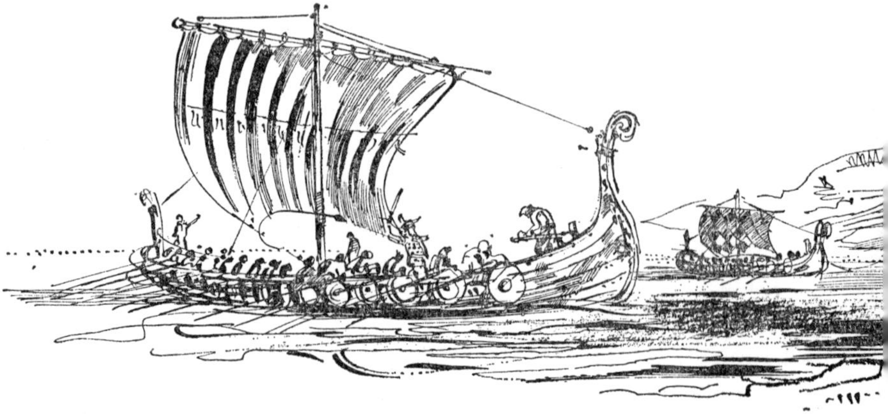

but I know it is not in you to kill a man. But all men, standing back to back in battle, must be ready to kill rather than see comrades killed."

The Skallings thronged the shore to see the longships sail. The day was fine and a breeze from the mountains filled out the sails – the red sail of Arnulf and the black sail of Sven, while four-score oars drove the ships even faster towards the headland and the open sea. The women wept, the little children whined, and the old men stood silent, recalling other times when they, too, had sailed, and those other warriors who had sailed with them and never returned.

Autumn came, the harvest was brought in. Crops were good and there was little fear for the winter. But one day the cattle began to fall ill and even the old women were at a loss to know what to do. Stiglaf took his staff and hobbled away into the hills and the marshland, hunting for days until he found the wandering people. The wise old woman who had once treated him when her people found him dying in the snow, now gave him herbs from her store and told him what must be done. The cattle were cured, save

one or two that were too weak already. The Skallings looked on Stiglaf with new respect, but also with a little fear. When winter had passed and the spring came again the old men came to consult Stiglaf about the crops and the cattle. It was as though they expected him to know how things should be ordered, just as his father had done. Stiglaf gave them his opinion, but gave no other sign of authority, speaking only when asked and still keeping to himself.

With the spring came news from the south. The war would be long and hard but the princes from beyond the southern sea would be driven back. The Northmen's ships were striking terror among the enemy forces. With the message were the names of three Skalling warriors who had died.

That summer was the worst for ten years. Gales tore the sea. High whirling winds threw down homes and cattle shelters. When the storms passed the rain followed and then low-hanging mist. The Skallings rescued what they could of their crops, but Stiglaf knew, even before the old men told him, that what had been harvested would not even last the winter, let alone provide food for the spring beyond.

And when the fish shoals proved to be poor and sparse, he knew that the future would be hard indeed.

Stiglaf pondered this problem for many days and finally made up his mind what he must do. In the early autumn, while there was still light and warmth, he set out again for the high rocks and marshland. After seven days' searching, he found the nomads with their herds and was greeted again by his friends. They made him welcome in their tents and he stood amazed at the gathering of the reindeer, stretching out across the plateau, their horns like a living forest.

When he had told his friends what his purpose was, they took him to their council, some dozen wizened yellow-brown-faced old men. They mulled over the matter for a while and then gave him their answer. He was their friend, though his people, the Skallings, had never been their friends. Yet they would help them with meat for the winter in exchange for the metal goods the Skallings were skilled in making. In return, they asked that if future winters should prove too hard for them on the plateau, they would be allowed to bring their beasts down to the lower slopes where the fodder was easier to find beneath the snow. Without hesitating, Stiglaf gave his word, for he knew that his father would approve of what he had done and would make sure the Skallings kept their part of the bargain.

So with Stiglaf's guidance, the Skallings lived through a second winter while their chiefs and their warriors were away. It was not easy and at times the food was short, but no one starved and the people were pleased enough with what Stiglaf had done, however suspicious they were of his friendship with the marshland nomads.

Spring came at last and as the ice broke on the lakes and

streams, word came from farther south that the ships were returning from battle. There was talk of fierce fighting, of deaths and of plunder, but no more than that. Stiglaf and the Skalling folk had to wait patiently. In April, with the sun rising higher in the sky, it was agreed that a constant watch should be kept from the rocky vantage point above the beach. The sharpest-eyed young people took turns in waiting from morning to evening.

One day, when April was nearly over, the longed-for cry of "Ships, ships!" was heard, and the people poured out from every homestead, heading for the shore. The oldest and feeblest among them had barely arrived to join the crowd when the two ships, the black sail of Sven and the red sail of Arnulf, swung round the headland and swept up the fjord, the great oars working and the ripples surging ahead of the dragon prows. The old men began to count in whispers as the oars rose and fell, flashing in the sunlight. There were eight oars missing from Arnulf's boat and twelve from Sven's. Twenty men dead or so wounded they could not pull an oar. It was a heavy toll, heavier even than the ill-fated voyage of the young men under Trygve, Eynor's son. But just how heavy the toll was, the Skallings had still to learn.

The red-sailed ship raced to shore first and over the gunwale sprang Torald, bulking huge in his worn and stained harness. He was followed more slowly by his father and the rest of his crew, leading or carrying back three badly wounded men, and last of all a tiny figure draped in black cloth. They marched triumphantly ashore and up the beach to the excited cheerings of the young Skallings, to be greeted by their families, while those whose men had not come back sought anxiously for news of them.

Amid the shouting and confusion, the black-sailed ship grounded its keel, and Stiglaf knew by some instinct that things had gone ill. First, weary and war-stained, came Eynor, followed by others of his crew. But of Sven and of Jofur and seven others there was no sign. The chief and his minstrel were gone.

Stiglaf felt the ice form round his heart. He could not weep as he had done when he was ten or twelve. He was now fourteen and a man – a fatherless man – a man who must bear all his burdens alone. He felt the rough and powerful arms of Eynor clasp him round the shoulders.

"Stiglaf, son of Sven, your father died as he lived, fighting for others to live. The Skallings have never known a greater man."

Eynor took from his clothes two small objects and pressed them into Stiglaf's hands. "Before the last battle, your father gave these to me and told me to carry them to you. They were your mother's gifts to him."

They were a small polished comb of wood, carved with tiny rune-like characters, something which Stiglaf had never seen before, and the silver brooch that Sven Forkbeard had always worn at his throat – in the shape of a snake curling round to take its tail into its own mouth.

The Skallings crowded round their returned warriors as they marched up the beach towards the fire hall, where the benches loaded with meat carefully kept from the winter rations were waiting.

But Stiglaf stayed there by the shore, gazing out over the water.

7

The Skallings gathered in the great hall as the sun went down. Men and women, even the older children, crowded in, filling the benches or squatting on the log floor. The great seat of Sven Fork-beard stood empty and Arnulf the Red chose to sit at the head of one table amid his own crew, with Torald at his side.

At the other main table sat Eynor with the men from Sven's ship. Eynor had urged Stiglaf to sit at the head of the table, but Stiglaf refused, finding a place nearer the foot of the table amid the older men who had stayed behind during the voyage.

Excitement was subdued now by the heavy feeling of loss. Sven had ruled the Skalling people for more than thirty years. No man living could remember his like, nor did the old stories tell of a mightier or a stranger man. It was held greatly to his honour that although he had not wished the Skallings to fight, rather than leave the warriors to venture leaderless into danger, he had gone at their head and had died far from his home.

Sigurd, skald of Arnulf, stood up and began to tell of the war, of the many battles against the princes of Serkland the Great. Their warriors, it was said, were dark as the night and their swords were not straight but curved like a crescent moon. Their arrow flights blotted out the sun and their ships could turn and twist like fish in the water.

There had been two great battles, sang Sigurd, when the ships were counted in hundreds and the fighting men by tens of thousands. And neither side could claim the victory. In the end the two foes had come to terms and the fighting had ended.

Then Sigurd came to the death of Sven, and as Stiglaf listened he became uneasy. It was as though behind Sigurd's story lay another story, but what it was he could not fathom.

At the close of the last battle, Arnulf and Torald and the men of their crew had sailed into an inlet pursuing a ship with some prince and his retainers on board. Seeing that the ship was richly laden, Arnulf's men had boldly pressed home the attack and driven the enemy ship aground, boarding it, wiping out the crew, ransacking the vessel and setting it on fire. But as they were about to retreat with their spoils, a large force of enemy soldiers had suddenly attacked them from the land. Arnulf's ship ran aground and was in danger of being overrun. Seeing this, Sven Fork-beard had sailed in to their aid. Turning his own ship, and bidding Eynor, with half the crew, use all their strength to haul off Arnulf's ship into deeper water, Sven had taken a score of his men and rushed on to the shore. There he fought off the attackers until both ships were clear. At the last he sent back most of his tiny rearguard force and with seven men only, astride a little passage through the rocks, he had held off the enemy. The Skalling ships had escaped, but Sven and his seven brave companions had all been cut down. Naming each of the seven and recording the worth and value of their families, Sigurd declared that three-score Skalling warriors, even the mighty Arnulf, brother of Sven, Torald his son, and Eynor, Sven's captain, owed their lives to the greatness of their chief.

Sven Fork-beard, mightiest of Skallings,
Leader of men, feeder of children,
When shall we see his like again?

Sigurd sang, and the Skallings, crowded into the great hall, murmured their agreement and sorrow. Silence spread through the company, rising into the greater silence beyond. Outside in the white water of the fjord, reflecting the milky white of the northern sky, only the ripples of rising fish disturbed the calm.

Through the open doorway drifted the faint scent of small flowers growing in the moss, and Stiglaf's heart seemed to rise and swell in his throat.

The boisterous sound of Torald's voice burst into his ears, as Arnulf's son, ignoring his father's warning glance, mounted upon the table in full view of all the Skallings and began to speak.

"Not all is sorrow and weeping. Many fell, but many more returned. The name of the Skallings and their fame has spread to Serkland the Great, where princes still speak of the dread sight of the red sail and the black. Cynewulf, captain of Harald Fine-hair, chose the red and the black to head his force each time we fell upon the dark hordes. He chose well and he paid well. We have brought back such riches, such gold and silver as Skalling eyes never saw before. In the lands of the south, the kings live not in cunningly carved halls of pine but in great white palaces, and their domes are covered in a net of gold."

He gestured to some of the young men in his father's

crew who ran to the corners of the hall to drag out chests and bundles which they opened to spill out a huge mound of brilliantly rich cloths and glittering ornaments, sword hilts, buckles, combs and clasps. They emptied one after another on to the glowing pile until the gasps of the crowd rose to shouts of amazement. Arnulf, who had tried to restrain his son at first, now smiled a thin smile of satisfaction. Only Eynor and the warriors around him remained silent.

But Torald had not finished yet. He ordered the young men to clear a space in the centre of the floor amid the heaps of plunder. When it was done, he spoke again, as if joking.

"There are Skallings who doubt our stories of the southern sea, some whose eyes are not convinced even by our treasures. How can it be, they say, that the people there are so dark, when here they are so fair?

"But as the day is light, so is the night dark. Even a child knows this. As half the year is dark night, so is half the world dark people, and as the day and the sun rise to triumph over the night and the dark, so have we conquered the dark princes and have returned among you to bring the glory and tell the tale."

Again he waved his hand for all the world as though he were a prince, thought Stiglaf. And two young men entered through the doorway, dragging between them the tiny dark-clad figure that Stiglaf remembered seeing taken from Arnulf's ship earlier that day.

They thrust the small figure into the space cleared amid the plunder. For a moment, left alone, the figure tried to stretch out its bound arms as though feeling for something secure in the emptiness around it. Then one of the young

men twitched away the black cloak and the Skallings stared in amazement.

"A girl," cried some. "No, a boy," shouted others.

Stiglaf stared at the slender creature in the crimson tunic decorated with gold edging, at the large eyes rolling white in the dark features beneath the shining black curls, at the thin arms and legs that trembled.

A little child, held in its mother's arms, screamed. Others giggled, chattered and pointed. The men and women argued among themselves until the noise of conversation became deafening. Stiglaf stared and stared and suddenly into his mind came the face of the nomad girl with her slant eyes and high cheek bones.

"Boy or girl, Torald, there is no need for you to fear.

Let your men cut the bonds," came the rough voice of Eynor, through the babble of voices.

A young man from Arnulf's band drew his knife and slit the thongs that held the prisoner's arms. Then he sprang back as the hands flashed out and left a thin trail of blood on his cheek.

With a gasp of rage he lunged back with his knife, aiming at the prisoner's side. The thick cloth of the tunic turned the blade aside, but the point must have scored the flesh beneath, for the mouth in the dark face opened and a strangled cry of pain, like that of a trapped animal, rang out.

There was a slithering and clacking sound. A shadow passed across the open door. The young man was seized by his neck and hurled with manic force across the log floor, to crash down beneath the table on which Torald still stood. In front of the prisoner, his light blue eyes glittering behind the fringe of yellow hair, his arms outstretched and his weight braced back on his sound leg, stood Stiglaf. His voice, high-pitched, pierced to the farthest corners of the hall. "Is this how your men gained victories over the Serklanders, Torald, with blade against unarmed children?"

Shocked into silence by the first words that Stiglaf had ever spoken before all men in the fire hall, the Skallings held their breath. First to break the spell was Torald. His face flushed with rage, he leapt down from the table, his hand reaching for his sword, then drawing back as his mind grasped the full meaning of Stiglaf's words. But as he moved, his father Arnulf rose and let his fist fall with a crash on the table before him till drinking vessels and bowls rattled.

"Torald, go to your place. There cannot be bad blood

between the sons of Sven and Arnulf. Stiglaf is right. It was a coward's trick and your man has suffered a coward's shame."

The men at both tables nodded their approval, but Arnulf had not done.

"Have no fear, Stiglaf. No man of mine shall harm the captive. And as a sign of the true friendship between your father and me, I give this slave into your keeping."

For a moment it seemed that Torald would protest, but he held his peace. Stiglaf nodded to Arnulf.

"I thank you, Uncle. I accept your gift. But on one condition. That Torald, my cousin, agrees and that he accepts that my words were spoken in anger at a coward's act and meant no insult to him, with whom I have no quarrel."

After a moment's hesitation, with all men's eyes on him, Torald nodded his head. Stiglaf took the captive by the shoulder and led the way out of the hall. As he left it seemed a weight was lifted from the air and Arnulf called out.

"Bring out the casks of wine we took from the prince's ship. Skalling warriors never tasted drink like this."

The noise, the shouting and singing rose into the white night and went on until dawn.

8

That night, Stiglaf's old servant Asbjorn, who had served Sven before him, brought out a thick skin robe to cover the still trembling body of the prisoner and told the child to lie down in a corner. But the poor creature only shivered more and refused to leave Stiglaf's side, sleeping at last, wrapped in the robe, close to Stiglaf in his own sleeping-place. Stiglaf brooded for a while over the events of the evening and the possible outcome of the enmity now openly shown between Torald and himself. Then he slept too, until the sun was high in the sky. He woke in alarm like a sleeper with bad dreams and looked around him. The robe lay tossed aside on the floor. The prisoner was gone.

He struggled to his feet, buckled his belt, took up his staff and limped to the doorway, calling for Asbjorn. But the old man had seen nothing. The captive must have gone past him like a shadow in the early hours. Or been taken? Surely there could not be such treachery? He went outside, but no one was about save old people and small children. Those who had not straggled away to the fields would still be lying in a drunken sleep.

Stiglaf hurried first to the shore and saw in the distance a little group of children gathered around something on the ground by the water's edge. As he came nearer, he saw the deep red colour of the captive's tunic in the middle of the circle of wide-eyed Skalling boys and girls. The thin dark fingers rose and fell, casting half a dozen bright pebbles from the sand in a swift juggling motion, then casting them in the clefts between the knuckles. Again the round stones rose in an arc, but this time they were snatched one by one from the air and spread out in a pattern on the ground.

Stiglaf pushed through the crowd of children and beckoned. For a moment the young captive hesitated and then, calmly and with a strange dignity, rose and followed him along the beach. He waved back the children when they tried to follow, and led the way round a turn in the shore-line into a sheltered gap in the rocks where they were alone. Then he turned and, signalling to his companion, he sat down on the sand. He looked keenly into the dark smooth features and the huge black eyes with their large whites, at the black ripples of the hair. Recalling the sign-talk with which he had spoken to the nomad people, he first smiled broadly and then placed his hand on his own chest.

"Stiglaf," he said. "Stiglaf."

He waited. For a moment it seemed that there would be no answer. Stiglaf repeated his name and smiled again. The large eyes slowly flooded and the tears began to flow down the dark cheeks. The slender hand rose to the chest of the red tunic. The muscles in the long throat worked and struggled as if choking, and from the open mouth came a strangled noise like the cry of pain given out by the captive the night before, but lower and softer. There were three sounds, each lower than the last, but they were not like the speech of men and women, but like the soft grunt or growl of an animal. This was not the language of a far-off land, Stiglaf knew this by instinct. It was the language of someone who could not speak. His companion was dumb. On an impulse, Stiglaf put out his own two hands and took the dark hands in his own, pressing and squeezing them again and again. For a while the tears went on flowing down the cheeks and chin and staining the crimson tunic. Then with a shake of the black hair, the weeping stopped.

Taking up a pointed shell, the captive began to draw in the sand just where the ebb and flow of the water left it smooth. First a landscape with trees, strange plants whose leaves sprouted from the top of the trunk and bent downwards; next a great domed building, then two lines of figures on either side of a great chair. With each figure or drawing came little noises, varying in pitch as though the voice were struggling to speak in a language it knew well but could not utter clearly. The drawing stopped as a bigger wave rushed up the beach and swept away the sketched figures. The captive shrugged and smiled briefly, then began to draw again. Once more the great chair and two lines of figures, which seemed to Stiglaf to represent warriors, each bearing over his shoulder the dreaded hooked swords of which Stiglaf had heard Sigurd the skald sing. Next a wall, and behind it other figures, smaller and less stiff, whose clothes blew about in an unseen wind. The captive looked shyly up at Stiglaf and then pointed first to the great figure seated on the chair and then to one of the smaller figures hidden behind the wall. Suddenly Stiglaf cried out in amazement and pointed to his companion.

Now he understood that the captive of the Skallings, the little black-hooded figure he had saved out of pity, was a girl, and the daughter of a prince. She read his understanding in his amazed glance and smiled again, this time broadly, her teeth flashing white in the smooth dark cheeks.

Stiglaf picked up a shell and began to draw in his turn. He drew a coastline and two ships locked in battle. Then a third approaching. The girl nodded quickly, several times to show she understood. Then he drew ships sailing away and on the shore a small band of men attacked by a larger, and, drawing one man larger than the rest, pointed to himself. She nodded once more vigorously and drew again the great figure from the throne, but now she showed him stretched out on the ground, and pointed to herself. And Stiglaf knew that she, too, like he, was alone.

They sat in silence as another wave washed up the beach and wiped out the signs of their past lives. Stiglaf stood up and, reaching down, took the girl's hand and drew her up. Together they walked along the beach and back to his home.

From that day on, through the summer she walked everywhere with Stiglaf, when he went to direct the work with the crops and the cattle, or with the small boats to get fish from the fjord, or on his wanderings through the woods. The Skallings grew accustomed to seeing the two together and, without a word from Stiglaf, began to treat her with silent respect, if not with liking. The little children ceased to stare at her or to follow her.

Eynor, seeing the way in which the people came to Stiglaf on matters concerning the growing of barley or the raising of the cattle, nodded his approval along with the old men. Torald, who paid no heed to crops or cattle, did not cross Stiglaf's path, and since Stiglaf went rarely to the great hall, their hostility stayed inside them and there was no open quarrel.

Arnulf, who was now head of the Skallings with Sven's death, kept to his home with a few companions. They passed the time in emptying one by one the casks of rare wine they had captured from the prince's ship. It was whispered that Arnulf was brooding over something. But since the summer weather was good and the harvest, both from land and sea, was plentiful, there was enough for all to do and little time for gossip. The families who had lost men on the last voyage began slowly to recover from their grief, and life in the valley seemed to return to the old ways.

Each morning early and evening, Stiglaf and the girl walked down to the shore.

There, in the language of pictures, they would talk together. She drew mysterious rune-like signs under each picture, and Stiglaf, a little ashamed that he had no writing to teach her, began to learn them. After some time he knew many of the signs so well that she no longer needed to draw pictures but would tell him what she wished in signs. Often she would take up his hand in hers and with her finger trace the outline of a sign on his palm, and he would do the same in her palm. He began to forget that she was dumb.

But he struggled to get her to pronounce her own name, repeating the strange sounds after her in many different ways until one day he said a word that made her clap her hands.

"Djamila."

Her mouth opened and she chuckled throatily and mouthed his name in her own way.

"Stig-laf."

Later as they walked up the rocky path from the cove to his home on the wood slope, they met Eynor. He turned

and walked silently with them. At the edge of the trees they were joined by three more of Sven's old crew and so, under escort, reached Stiglaf's home. There was a strange quiet throughout the homesteads as though people were waiting for something. When Djamila had gone inside, Eynor beckoned to Stiglaf to follow him and, leaving two men on guard outside the doorway, walked down towards the wide beach where the longships were always moored. Only then did Eynor speak, quietly and urgently.

"Listen, Stiglaf. Arnulf is going to die. This morning he could not wake. Even the wisest of the old women do not know what illness has struck him. But they found in one small cask of wine, the smallest and best, which Arnulf kept for himself, a strange powder mixed with the lees. They fear he has been poisoned.

"If that is so, then the girl's life is no longer safe, even under your care."

Stiglaf frowned: "This is foolishness. There is no poison. Arnulf has drunk so much since the ships came back his body sickens. Let him sleep and the illness will pass."

Eynor shrugged: "I have warned you, Stiglaf. And remember I am your father's man and your true friend. But Arnulf is still head of the Skallings after Sven Fork-beard. And Torald longs to take his place. He is as cruel as his father and not as wise."

Next day, Arnulf came to his sense, but did not leave his bed. His illness left him too weak to move, though not too weak to curse or plot. For some days he brooded, turning restlessly in his sleeping-place, grumbling when the passing of time did not bring back his old strength. So things went on until the summer began to draw to an end. Then Arnulf called for Eynor and the veterans from both ships as well as the old men. He sent for Stiglaf too, and when the young man limped quietly over Arnulf's threshold, he found some dozen men, including the red-headed Torald, gathered round Arnulf's bed. Stiglaf was stunned to see how thin his uncle, always lean and wolf-like, had become, and how the bearded skin, stretched tight over his cheekbones, showed white and death-like. The voice was no longer harsh and rasping, but strained and feeble. Arnulf raised his hand, drooping at the wrist. Stiglaf looked keenly at him and knew with a sinking heart that this was no ordinary sickness. There was death and danger in the air.

Said Arnulf: "I have told my men to build my death-ship. They must build fast because I have not many days more. The princes from below the southern sea have had the last laugh and struck the last blow. It was a deadly trick, to leave one poisoned jar among so much sweet wine. They have had their revenge."

Torald seemed about to speak, but his father silenced him with a turn of his head.

"We must talk over what shall happen after I am gone on my last voyage. Who shall lead the Skallings?"

An old man said: "It is for a full meet in the fire hall to decide that."

Arnulf nodded, his head wagged feebly. His voice suddenly took on the cunning tone so renowned when he spoke in council.

"The matter is not easy. We may take counsel before that so there shall be no strife in the full meet." The others nodded, there was wisdom here. Now the oldest of the men present, a bent figure whose still rosy cheeks glowed amid shaggy white hair that hung down to his shoulders, spoke:

"By custom, there is not need for choice, or strife. By right, Stiglaf, son of Sven, should be leader."

Others murmured their agreement, but there was a movement among the group and Torald thrust his face forward close to that of his father. He whispered harshly: "But it is foreseen that Stiglaf shall never lead the Skallings."

"What does Torald say?" demanded Eynor suspiciously. Arnulf heaved himself up, half-sitting, his eyes crafty. "Torald says nothing. I know . . ." he turned to the oldest man. "I know the worth of Stiglaf, Sven's son, how even the oldest takes his word on matters of weight. But I do not do him wrong when I say that a chief of the Skallings must not only be cunning in the ways of feeding and clothing his people. He must also lead them in war. That, too, must be weighed, and in matters of war there can be no doubt that Torald my son is skilled and has won praise from older men."

Eynor and the other warriors nodded. Arnulf went on:

"It is not easy to decide and I have thought much about it. My counsel is that Stiglaf and Torald should rule together, taking heed one of the other, the one skilled in peace, the other in war, and aided by the wisdom of the older men."

Eynor spoke: "Your word is good, Arnulf, but paths do not run straight through the forest. Who shall give the word for peace or war?"

Arnulf nodded: "In such matters, Eynor, while the chiefs are still young, then you must be their guide. I can speak no more now, let this counsel be ended."

9

The death-ship of Arnulf the Red, rigged with mast and stern oar, but without sweeps and far smaller than the old warrior's longship, lay moored in the shallows. It was already loaded with his weapons and harness, with rich goods taken from his last voyage and voyages before. A thick bearskin lay on the deck before the mast. All that lacked now was the body of Arnulf who lay slowly dying.

Stiglaf went about his own business, for it was harvest-time and every man and woman was in the fields below the forests, cutting and binding, making ready the place for threshing and winnowing. As the weather had promised, the crops were good and the winter could be easy with no hunger for the Skallings. It would be the first winter in three that the young warriors were at home with their families. But the Skallings must face this winter knowing that neither Sven nor Arnulf would walk among them again. The people watched the two sons – Stiglaf as he limped around the fields or along the shore-line, Torald as he paced impatiently around his father's home – and wondered what their lives would be like under the double rule of two men so unlike.

The young girl Djamila was seen no more. Stiglaf had told her to stay within doors and had asked Asbjorn to keep a close eye that no harm came to her while he was away. Djamila did not complain. Though she was a princess in her own land, it seemed her hands were skilful and she sat with the women in Sven's old home and spun and wove together with them. She listened while they sang old songs and murmured her own tunes between her teeth. And sometimes she fell silent and looked into the distance. The women watched her but did not try to talk to her, only looking curiously and suspiciously as she spoke to Stiglaf by tracing signs on his hand or in the earth. If they had thoughts about her they kept them to themselves.

It was not simply that Stiglaf might hear and be angry, but they guessed that though Djamila might be dumb, her eyes and ears were sharp. How did they know she did not understand their words and would know their secrets? There was much about Djamila that was mysterious, and the story of the wine cask which had brought death to Arnulf across the ocean had spread among the Skallings. But Djamila was under Stiglaf's protection.

One evening, when the harvest was nearly in, Stiglaf came towards his father's house. He walked with his head down, thinking deeply, and did not see until he came near the door that his way was barred. Before him stood Torald and two of his men, one of them the tormentor of Djamila, whom Stiglaf had humiliated that night in the great hall. Now he gazed at Stiglaf with eyes of hate. Torald spoke:

"Stiglaf, son of Sven. I have things to say to you."

"If that is so," replied Stiglaf quietly, "then send your men away and let us walk among the trees and talk. I will not speak with you in front of them."

For a moment it seemed the men would refuse to go, but Torald waved his arm and told them to wait farther down the path. Then he spoke again, slowly and clenching his teeth.

"My father will be dead by to-night. To-morrow morning he will sail on his death-ship. His death has been caused by the witch you protect and I demand her death in return, as custom and law provide."

Fear gripped Stiglaf's heart, but his voice was calm:

"The girl is no witch, but a lady among her own people, and her father is a prince and a brave warrior. Your father knew that, if you do not. She has not killed your father, but if she had then by law and custom she had a right. Your ship-men killed her father and took her prisoner."

Torald spat: "Then she is our prisoner and we shall do as we will with her."

"By the word of your father she is no more your prisoner, but in my care. Shall it be known among the Skallings that you went against your father's word before his body was cold?"

"Shall it be known among the Skallings that Stiglaf, son of Sven, sheltered a witch who brought about the death of Sven's brother? I demand her and I shall have her."

"Then you must first kill me."

Torald threw back his head and laughed.

"Do you think I won't? Do you think I'll be quiet and share the rule of the Skallings with a cripple who dare not sail beyond the mouth of the fjord? You will never rule the Skallings. It is foreseen that you shall not."

These last words rushed from Torald's mouth before he could halt them, but Stiglaf grasped their meaning.

"How can you know what is foreseen for me? Who has told you? What treachery is this?"

Torald shrugged. "Why should I keep the secret which I

had from my father. In the days before we were born, Sven Fork-beard went to Unna, the old woman of the hills, and asked her what was foreseen for you. He did not care for what he heard and kept it to himself. But my father followed him there and heard all."

"Your father spied on mine? Brother spied on brother?"

"Yes, and I will tell you what your father did not dare tell you. What Unna told him, he dared tell no one for he hoped to avoid fate and have you rule the Skallings despite what is foreseen. I will tell you what Unna said:

" 'Stiglaf, son of Sven, will be a cripple among cripples.

" 'Stiglaf, son of Sven, will never rule the Skallings.

" 'Stiglaf, son of Sven, will bring his line to an end.' "

The two cousins faced one another on the rocky path, Stiglaf with his back to the sea. Torald leaned forward.

"With one thrust I could send you over into the water where you will drown and no one will know, only my men watching among the trees up there."

Stiglaf braced himself on the path by his good leg and replied:

"Thrust, then, Torald, thrust away. Murder me as you mean to murder Djamila. But do you think you will escape your own fate? Do you know what Unna foresaw for you?"

Torald shouted triumphantly.

"Yes, I know. I shall rule the Skallings."

"Is that all Unna foresaw for you?"

"No, I shall be a true son of my father and carry death to the southern seas and back."

"As your father did?"

A shadow passed over Torald's face and was gone, though not before Stiglaf had seen it.

"Is that all Unna foresaw for you?" demanded Stiglaf.

"Yes, that I shall rule the Skallings!" shouted Torald defiantly. But his voice dropped. "See, Stiglaf, I do not wish your death. I will not kill your witch but leave her to keep you company. All I ask is that you accept me as ruler of the Skallings, as it is foreseen."

Stiglaf laughed: "If it is foreseen, then my poor help will be no use to you. But I make no bargains with men like you. I knew you before as a boaster, but a bold warrior. Now I know you as a traitor and a man with murder in his heart."

Stepping forward suddenly, Stiglaf pushed past Torald and walked up the path towards his home. As he went he heard Torald's voice, full of hate:

"With those words, you put the knife to your own throat."

Late that evening, Stiglaf went to Djamila and, leading her into his own room, he took her hand and traced on her palm his urgent message.

"Djamila. You are in danger. To-morrow, before they launch the death-ship, I will lead you to a hiding-place. Later I will take you to my friends in the hills. They will protect you."

She answered: "I will not leave you."

"You must. Do not be afraid for me. Do as I say, and in the end all will be well. Stay close indoors and old Asbjorn will guard the door."

He left her and went to the home of Eynor and told the warrior all that had been said. Eynor spoke frankly.

"Stiglaf, you must not divide the Skallings over a stranger. No good can come of that. If you can take her away to safety, do so. But do not bring her back. Above all, take care for the future. You may be forced to kill Torald or else he will kill you. His father schemed to have his son lead the Skallings, but he has not murdered to do this. Torald has a heart of ice and will kill you if he has to. I will stand by you and there are others among the warriors who will be your friends for your father's sake. But do not force Skalling to fight Skalling."

Stiglaf left Eynor and went out into the forest. The thought that he might one day be forced to kill his own cousin if Djamila's life or his own were to be safe, burned in his mind like a hot ember. Perhaps if his present bad time could be lived through by skill and cunning, the horrible choice might be avoided. He wandered through the dim, grey night and finally exhausted with his thoughts, he lay down on the moss beneath the bush and slept heavily.

He was awakened by the sun burning into his eyes, and looked wildly about him. How long had he slept? He struggled to his feet and, cursing his lame leg, he staggered in a broken run down the path towards the Skalling homesteads. The fields as he passed were empty. No man, no woman was at work, though the sun was high. A panic seized him and he stumbled on muttering Djamila's name.

The doorway to his home stood open. No one was about, even the women had disappeared. From inside rose a faint sound of groaning as though someone were in pain. Searching feverishly he tracked down the sound to the room where Djamila had lain. On the floor, curled up in agony, his old head streaming with blood, lay Asbjorn. The old man's eyes turned up to his, in distress, and in broken words he told what had happened, only an hour before Stiglaf's return.

In the early hours, while the sun was still only half risen, some treacherous member of the household had silently admitted three of Torald's crew men. They had overpowered Asbjorn after a desperate struggle, had seized Djamila, who could not cry out, and were gone in a moment before others in the house were aware of the betrayal.

"Where have they taken her?" asked Stiglaf. But he already knew. Leaving the old man leaning heavily against the wall, Stiglaf took his staff and hurried down towards the shore. Even as he cleared the trees, he could see the beach crowded with people, young and old, a great throng down to the water's edge and even wading into the water. In the death-ship, dressed in his finest harness which twinkled and gleamed in the sun, his great red cloak on his shoulders, was the body of Arnulf, as if he were commanding the oarsmen. As Stiglaf reached the edge of the crowd. Arnulf's crew men set the boat afloat. They held it in the shallows lest the current carry it away.

But now they were ready. The crowd parted at the water's edge.

Stiglaf saw three of Arnulf's ship-men carry Djamila, her crimson tunic like blood against the sand, and push her over the gunwale of the death-ship.

''Stop, Skallings, stop! This is murder!" called Stiglaf. Heads turned in the crowd and the crew men at the shore seemed to hesitate. But Torald urged them on and, plunging into the water, helped them push the death-ship out into the clutching current.

Then came more horror. As Djamila crouched down near the mast, Torald and his companions took lighted torches and threw them on to the stern of the ship. Blazing, it drifted away down the fjord.

10

The sight of the flames shooting above the stern of the death-ship, and the cloud of smoke that suddenly covered the body of Arnulf and the cowering figure of Djamila, maddened Stiglaf. Raising his staff, he rushed forward, striking blindly left and right. People stumbled out of his way, bewildered by his onslaught and frightened by the mad blaze in his blue eyes. From the other side of the swirling crowd of men, women and children, Torald and his ship-men, armed and in full harness, turned from the water and advanced towards him. Women and children caught in the middle began to scream and cry, and the older men shouted vainly "Peace, no fighting!"

Stiglaf had gone forward several paces on his first rush when his arms were seized from behind in a grip as powerful as a mountain bear's. In his ear sounded the low, harsh voice of Eynor.

"Stiglaf, hold. This is death. They mean to kill you and this is their chance."

Stiglaf struggled violently, but Eynor had trapped his arms and the staff dropped from his writhing fingers. The crowd still milled around and Torald and his men still pushed their way between the women and children, throwing them to one side as they came up the beach. As he saw the whimpering children pushed to the ground, Stiglaf's rage changed to fear, but not fear for himself. He had gone beyond that. While he vented his fury on his fellow Skallings, the burning boat with Djamila and her grim companion was swinging in the current past the great rock. Soon it would reach the outer headland and the open sea, where, burnt to the water line, it would sink, a blackened hissing wreck, into the grey waters. Then he knew what he must do. In the farther inlet lay his own small boat which he used when fishing in the fjord. If he could reach and launch it, he might still cheat Torald of his revenge and save Djamila.

He tried again to break loose, but Eynor still held him.

"Quiet, Stiglaf. My men, your father's old comrades, are around us. Torald will not dare touch you now, if you say no more. The dark maid cannot be saved. The smoke will smother her and she will feel nothing. Death will not be hard on her."

Stiglaf's body became limp as though he were very tired. The old warrior's grasp relaxed and fell away. In a flash Stiglaf stooped, snatched up his staff, leaping backwards. Eynor tried to take hold of him again, but Stiglaf thrust his staff into the older man's belly. Made agile by desperation, Stiglaf dodged among the warriors and headed for the great lookout rock, leaping, hopping, stumbling, working his staff like a paddle. Then he thrust his staff between his teeth and hauled himself from grass tuft to jutting stone, taking the straight way up the rock-face. The crowd stood for a moment unable to see what he was after. But Torald, shrewd in his fury, saw quickly.

"Round to the inlet. Seize the cripple's boat," he shouted.

As Stiglaf reached the top of the rock he looked down.

In the midst of the crowd a confused struggle was going on between Eynor's and Torald's men, while the older men and women vainly tried to separate the two groups. But two or three of Torald's men had broken away and were running along the shore to skirt the rock and reach the farther inlet by the path at the edge of the woods. Stiglaf clenched his teeth. He could beat them yet. He would jump like a goat down the rock-face to the sand and have the small boat in the water before they could round the point

He sprang forward. But his lame leg twisted and crumpled beneath him. His body went headlong, somersaulted and rolled. Shoulders and head struck the jagged rock with sickening force as he fell towards the edge.

As he felt the ground vanish beneath him, he had a moment's vision of the death-ship, wrapped in smoke and flames, in the grip of the current, whirling by below. Then he was falling, falling.

Half-dazed by his efforts and the blows from the rocks, Stiglaf did not struggle, but dropped like a stone, plunging into the water and down into its cold, black depths. His breath froze in his lungs, and in his mind, as the waters closed over him, was the sight of the ship and the two still bodies.

His legs, as if they had their own life, began to kick and lunge. His arms flung about desperately. Each part of his body seemed to be fighting for its own right to live. The black water above and around him was suddenly pierced by a bright ball of sunlight and then, gasping and choking, his head shot above the water, driven by his madly whirling limbs. As his weight began to draw him down again, a dark shape passed between him and the sun, like a giant fish in the water. By blind instinct, Stiglaf's long left arm

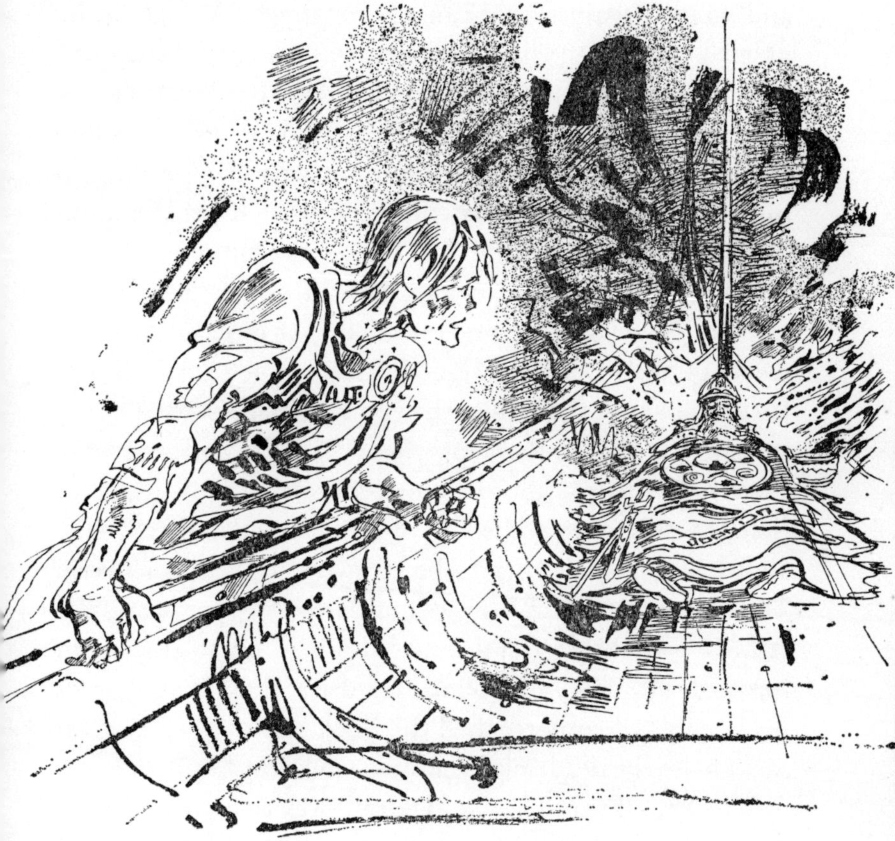

struck out and took hold, gripping, while his shoulder joints took the strain and he was dragged along half in, half out of the water.

From the pain of his clutching fingers, the message went to his brain. With terrible effort, the muscles, long hardened and strengthened by climbing in the forests and hills, answered the call. His right arm reached out, following the line of the left, and took hold. Now he heaved his sodden body clear of the water and felt new pain as his chest struck and scraped against hard timber. Flinging back his hair, he opened his eyes to the bright sun and his lungs to the air. In an instant he was choked and blinded as a cloud of black smoke swept down. Spurred by a sudden understanding of where he was, he gave one more straining heave, and his body, limp and exhausted, swung over the side and on to the smouldering timbers of the death-ship.

Sparks and embers stung his bare arms and legs, singed his hair. New waves of smoke rolled over him, followed by waves of heat. But now he could see and act more clearly. He had boarded the ship at the bows. The fire, started in the stern of the ship, was creeping forward. The midships were obscured by smoke, but he could see with one swift glance that only the sides and some of the deck planks were well alight. Holding his breath, he struggled back to the mast. The sun vanished and he was in darkness. The heat grew stronger. Grabbing for the mast he held on to it and felt forward with his right hand. He drew back in disgust as his fingers suddenly reached the thick hair that fell in great locks from the dead chief's helmet. Choking, he changed his grip to Arnulf's shoulder and felt his way again, walking his fingers down the arm to the stiff fingers where they rested on the hip, then down the cloth and leather-thonged leg to the stitched sandals and the deck below. He dropped on one knee and, leaning against the dead man's side, spread out both arms and began to feel frantically around him. Nothing.

Clenching his fists to fight away panic, he turned to the gunwale. He could not go much farther astern, because the heat was growing. He reached the side of the ship. Nothing. Now desperate, he turned and crawled on hands and knees that winced and jerked as hot fragments of wood touched them towards the other side. He found Djamila's body curled up as though she were asleep. The skirt of the red tunic had begun to smoulder from falling sparks. The smell of singeing rose from the black curls.

He thrust his arms under hers and heaved the body past the mast and into the bows. Slipping his fingers through the opening at the neck of her tunic, he felt the girl's smooth skin and beneath it the faint whispering beat of her heart. Djamila was alive.

On his feet again, he pushed his way towards the mast, more surely now that he made the journey for the second time. And now he knew where to look. He reached Arnulf's side again, but this time no feeling of horror held him back. He thrust the chief's legs to one side and found what he wanted – a deep, carved metal vessel. He chuckled grimly to himself. If Arnulf did not wish his nephew's death in the way Torald did, then he would not be angry if his goods were borrowed. Then to the side of the ship. Hanging over the gunwale and letting the iron pot hang at the end of his arms, he could reach the water. The first cauldron-full was badly aimed and the foul puff of smoke half blinded him. But the second found its mark. Flames died, the blackened wood sizzled, the smoke rose and died away. Now he inched his way towards the stern, heaving up the cauldron and hurling the water on the flames, then moving forward again. Bending, stretching, pouring, turning, he moved quickly but calmly. The ship would not burn. Indeed, as he reached the stern and quenched the last flicker of flame, he could see that the damage was not great. Even the stern oar was only partly burnt away down half its length and could still be used. Every plank for half the ship's length was charred, but the ship still held water.

Pushing past Arnulf, he went to the bows and found that Djamila had begun to open her eyes. Eagerly he bent down and cleaned her face of the soot and grime and splashed water in her face. Now her eyes opened wide and took in his face. Her look of astonishment slowly gave way to one of pleasure and the red lips opened in a smile.

Reassured now, Stiglaf looked out beyond the ship. It had reached the narrow strait, sheltered by the outer headland, that led to the open sea. All at once he realised that he, who had never made a voyage beyond the fjord and knew little of navigating, would have to learn and learn quickly.

For there could be no going back to the valley of the Skallings after what he had done. To board a death-ship and put out the flames, to hurl the body of his uncle from its place, was a crime that could not be forgiven by the dead man's family, indeed it was an offence to the whole Skalling people. There could be no going back. He must sail his little ship with its strange passengers to wherever wind and wave might lead them. Sail? The ship had no sail. Then he must go where tide and current would take him. Perhaps when they reached the open sea, the great stream from the south-west would bring them back to shore. But if they landed to the north, perhaps he could find a safe resting-place there.

Stiglaf turned to make his way back to the stern. As he passed his uncle's body again, he straightened the corpse and pulled the great red cloak more closely round it, turning one corner to cover the pale face and red beard and the staring eyes. Then he laid the body down by the mast, facing bow to stern, and rearranged the goods that had been stowed around the corpse's feet. He saw to his satisfaction that these included not only ornaments, but lines and hooks, small pins and knives, much that was useful to keep Djamila and himself alive.

"We shall be your guests, Uncle," he murmured, and turned again to go to the stern oar.

But as he did there came a strange, choked cry from Djamila, whose bare feet came rushing down the length of the ship. She seized his arm and pointed over to the nearer shore, to the inlet beyond the great rock. Boats were putting out from the land, forced through the water by straining oarsmen. Two were heading towards the strait, seeking to cut them off. One headed directly for the ship, and even at this distance Stiglaf could see the tall form of Torald erect in the bows. This he might have foreseen.

To have believed they would be allowed to drift out quietly to sea and safety was foolish. Torald would have his revenge, and Stiglaf had saved Djamila from an easy death, perhaps to suffer a harder one. Silently cursing his own rashness, he watched the pursuing boats surge forward, pause and surge forward again with each stroke of the oars. The death-ship, still caught in the current, still slipping towards the open sea, seemed to stand still in the water as the pursuers reached out on either side and closed in. Now the face and features of Torald, framed in his flowing red hair, the lips curled wolfishly, stood out more clearly as the distance lessened. Across the ripples in the water of the fjord came his voice.

"Stiglaf! Throw the witch into the water. Let her meet her fate and I will forget the insult to my father. Throw her over the side or I swear that both of you will feed the fishes."

Stiglaf bent down and reached for Arnulf's spear which

had fallen from the dead chief's grasp. Then he stood up high in the stern, bracing his foot against the stern oar and holding up the ash-shaft with its broad blade in a gesture of defiance. It was a useless gesture and he knew it. Torald laughed.

"Are you ready to draw blood, then, Stiglaf the Unsteady?"

The boatmen turned their heads and they laughed in their turn. Their laughter echoed across the water as they heaved more strongly on the oars. Stiglaf heard them with a heavy heart. He felt a fresh breeze down from the hills, carrying a faint scent of pine. The cool draught of air struck on his heated face. Slowly his mind became calm and he forced his gaze to meet the grinning face of his cousin. He waited. Again the breeze gusted and he felt the death-ship heave beneath his feet. Again the breeze and again the rocking motion.

This time it came in a surge and made him brace his feet harder against the stern oar. His glance fell and caught the ripples of water that spread behind the ship and glided back to meet the smaller prow of Torald's boat.

What was Torald about? Why was he holding back? Stiglaf's baffled mind could not grasp it, but his eye told him that in the brief moment since Torald had shouted to him, the distance between the two craft had not lessened. It was as though they were held apart by magic. Stiglaf wiped the sweat-damp from his face and strained his eyes. Was it a trick of the sun, that Torald's face, fixed in the middle distance, did not come any closer?

Once again the death-ship dipped and heeled beneath his feet. Again the ripples spread out beyond the stern. There was something strange here and he could not make it out. Now it seemed almost as though the figure of Torald was moving away from him. A sound escaped Torald's lips. It was not laughter now, but rage. Torald turned to his crew, shouting furiously, urging them to pull harder on their oars. But still they slipped back. Torald turned back to face Stiglaf, raised his arm, shook his fist and shouted again. But now Stiglaf could barely tell what his cousin was shouting. His mind was elsewhere, taken with the sudden knowledge that the ship he stood on was moving faster, faster than the current could take it, moving in swoops like a bird gliding on the wing. Now he could understand what Torald was shouting.

"The witch, the witch!"

Unable to believe what his sense told him, and still suspecting some magic, Stiglaf slid down from his perch on the stern oar. He turned to face the bows. The ship was under sail. He brushed his hand across his eyes as if to clear the vision from them. But it was true.

The ship, now gathering speed, was borne along by a red sail.

And beneath the mast, as in days of old, his eyes staring into the far reaches of the open sea, sat Arnulf the Red.

11

Stiglaf halted, stood stride-legged in the centre of the ship, and faced his uncle. He gripped the old warrior's spear and stared again. The eyes stared coldly back at him, the long fingers grasped the hilt of the sword at his side. Stiglaf waited for the lips to open and speak, to tell him what had happened and how the ship had suddenly sprouted sail to carry him away from danger.

But no words came. Stiglaf started forward. His hand stretched out and touched his uncle's face. It was stiff and cold. His uncle was as dead as ever he had been. But how then . . . and why . . . ?

From forward, beyond the billowing scarlet sail, came a soft grunting chuckle. Stiglaf, still bewildered, ducked beneath the sail and ran into the bows. There, sitting cross-legged on the lookout's platform, her back against the curved arch of the dragon figurehead, was Djamila, white teeth gleaming. She held her arms crossed over her stomach and chuckled. Before Stiglaf could prevent it, the words burst from him.

"What magic have you made, Djamila?"

She chuckled still more and, rising, took him playfully by the hand and led him back to the stern. There she took his hand and laid it on the stern oar. For a moment he stared at her stupidly, then he understood. Now that the ship was in the open sea, it had begun to roll. The red sail began to droop. Stiglaf threw his weight on to the oar and slowly the little ship slid round, the sail bloomed and the vessel went forward heading into the west. Djamila took his sleeve between her fingers and with her other hand pointed forward. Stiglaf stared and stared; and slowly he began to understand. His eyes went to the body of his uncle sitting rigidly upright before the mast. And he remembered how he had quelled the fire and laid his uncle down, wrapped in his own red cloak.

But now the cloak, a huge piece of cloth big enough for two men, floated above them as a sail. It had been lashed to the spars by leather thongs slashed from his uncle's legs with one of his own knives. While Stiglaf had been standing rigid and defiant, spear in hand, making his empty gesture of defiance to Torald, Djamila had dragged up the body of Arnulf, stripped off the cloak and had climbed like a monkey to the head of the mast to tie the cloak in place. In the old days, so Stiglaf had been told, before the longships were rigged for sail, the crew men had held up their cloaks to catch the wind and ease the burden of rowing. This dumb girl, whom he had tried to protect, had saved him. They were equal now – his life for hers. His arms round the stern oar, his face open to the breeze, his eyes on the red sail, Stiglaf began to laugh.

He laughed and laughed for sheer happiness and delight in life. The day that had begun so desperately for both of them had brought better things. Nothing that lay before them, he thought, could be worse, or more dangerous, than what they had passed through.

Torald and his band were left far behind. Even if they

launched the longship, they would be hard put to find them, let alone catch up with them. To search the wide sea in the darkness would be like hunting for one twig in the forest. They were safe and free to go where they cared. He felt no ties now binding him to the Skallings since they had thrust Djamila on to the death-ship. Even Eynor, his old friend and companion of his father, had tried to persuade him to let the girl die. And who was there to think of him now that his father had gone to join his mother?

He looked at the girl who sat near him, leaning her back against the beams of the ship and crooning a strange song-like noise to herself.

"Djamila," he called. She turned.

"Does your mother still live?"

The girl drew closer to him and, taking his hand, wrote her answer on his hand with her finger.

"My mother lives and my brother and sisters too."

"Shall we go and find them?"

The girl smiled wistfully and answered.

"The sun would rise and set more times than you could count before we could return there, even if we could find the way. We might die long before we came there."

"Then where shall we sail?"

"The wind blows us towards the sun. Let us go where it blows."

"Over the sea, where the sun goes down, lie the islands from where my father took my mother many years ago."

"But they are your foes."

"They cannot be more cruel than my own people," said Stiglaf.

When night fell, they took the great stone that served as anchor and lashed it to the great stiff body of Arnulf the

Red. They attached the richest ornaments to it, keeping back only the spear and the small knives and hooks. Straining and heaving together, they rolled it over the side and into the sea. It sank with hardly a splash, and the last of the Skalling chiefs was gone forever. Stiglaf pondered over the old man and the evil he had done. But his life had not been all evil, perhaps, and Arnulf had proved less cruel and vengeful than Torald his son.

He leaned on the swaying stern oar and listened to the flap of the sail in the night wind. By his side, Djamila slept restlessly. Daylight found him dozing over the tiller. A fair breeze still swelled the sail and the sun now rose in the sky behind them. They were alone on the sea. The land of the Skallings lay over the eastern horizon and no land appeared before them.

Among the goods that had been stacked around Arnulf's body they found a little food, dried meat and fish. It would last a few days if they ate sparingly. Djamila took one of the small knives and cut the food into tiny squares. They made their first meal together in silence and then the girl took the stern oar while Stiglaf lay on the bow platform in the mild sun and slept till midday. In the afternoon he strung a line with hooks, baited them with some of their precious food and trailed it in the water. Three hours' fishing brought four small fish which they ate raw, and so the day passed, and the next.

On the third day the dawn rose grey and murky and the waves began to mount. The sun ran behind the clouds and rain fell in squalls. With great presence of mind, Djamila set out the iron cauldron by the mast and caught water to quench their thirst. But they had little to eat that day. There was no fishing, and when the night came there was no sleep for the two of them needed all their strength to keep the ship's prow into the waves that bore down on them. By dawn the next day they were exhausted, but the storm went on. They were being driven from their westward course and forced to turn to the south-west. But the ship was like a swan in the water. It was so well made that the dragon prow rode the waves, plunging down and rising up again. Only when the two young sailors, worn out by lack of sleep, could not hold the boat steady and the stern oar was dragged from their grasp, did sea-water rush aboard. Stiglaf tried to secure the oar with braided thongs, but they snapped again and again. For four days and nights more they hung on, steadying the course of the boat. They longed for rest, but never dared lie down. Their clothes sodden, their shoulders raw, their faces grimed and salt-crusted, they clung to the stern oar and to each other. When the storm was at its height, they linked their belts together so that they should not be swept apart if the sea overwhelmed the ship. So they passed the seventh and the eighth day.

Relief came when they could hold out no longer. Both had sunk into a deep sleep while the tail of the storm passed over them and hurried away to the south. Stiglaf opened his eyes to the gleam of the sun, light blue sky and wispy white clouds high above them. The ship's planks were awash and the few remains of Arnulf's death goods rolled and clattered as the ship swung to and fro. But the sea was calmer.

They struggled to their feet, hungry and thirsty, and began to bale out the boat. Then Stiglaf baited the fishing hooks with the last of their miserable scraps of food and trailed them over the side. Djamila went forward and perched herself on the lookout platform, her keen eyes searching the horizon ahead. The fish would not bite and Stiglaf watched the water despondently, his spirit drained from him by the fight with the sea. Death, he mused, did not care to be cheated and always came again to claim victims he had lost unfairly.

He was so deep in thought that he did not hear Djamila call him. But suddenly she stood by him and shook him by the shoulder. As his head jerked up, the girl pointed away over the side of the ship. There, low on the horizon, like a thin cloud, was land. And as Stiglaf staggered to his feet rubbing his eyes, the line jerked. Too late he clutched for it. The fish that bit was away, making a meal of their food instead of providing them with a meal.

But the sight of land so raised his spirits that even this could not depress him again. Taking a firm grip on the stern oar, Stiglaf fought down the pain of hunger and thirst inside him and fixed his eyes on the land that slowly but surely drew nearer.

12

Stiglaf gazed in wonder as the ship, its red sail still filled by a stiff breeze, drove nearer and nearer to the land. To a Skalling, land meant mountains rising jagged and grand, sheer from the water's edge, fringed with narrow bands of rock where sea-lions slithered and dozed. It meant dark pine woods, streaked with silver and reddish-gold from the autumn birches. But here were no mountains, only a gentle slope of land away from the sea, a curving bay where the waves broke gently, and beyond the shore the round green shapes of trees.

He strained his eyes, turning his head slowly from north to south and scanned the line of shore and the woods. But he could see no sign of life, not even the smallest wisp of smoke to show that humans lived there. This was to the good, he thought, for men who lived on these islands might have a harsh welcome for uninvited guests sailing in from the sea. He leaned on the oar and carefully guided the ship towards the bay. There was no difficulty in this, for the entrance was wide and the water deep with no rocks. But as they came closer inland, he began to feel the tug of a tide beneath the keel. This was good. If he could sail with the tide as far up the beach as the water would carry and ground the keel, then when the tide went out it would leave their craft secure until it turned again. This would give them time to land and hunt for food, then fall back to the sea if need be. He turned and spoke quietly and briefly to Djamila, who nodded without a word.

The tide carried them on and the wind dropped. In surges the water bore the ship on, while Stiglaf's weight on the stern oar kept the prow straight. A dozen times it seemed they would ground, but each time the retreating sea bore them back, until at last with a jar that shook the timbers, the keel burrowed into the sand, the ship listed, and the two had to clutch wildly to hold their balance. But they were firmly grounded and the ship was unharmed.

Stiglaf took up the spear and Djamila thrust the knife Arnulf had left into her tunic. They dropped into the water up to their waists and waded up the sloping beach. The shore was fine and smooth, peppered white with shells and strewn with seaweed. Stiglaf knew at a glance that if the woods yielded no game, then the pools on the shore would give them food.

With this thought, his hunger, not satisfied for days, rose again, but so did his spirits. To be alive, to be on dry land again was enough for the present. He grinned at Djamila, who grinned back, and they set off up the beach towards the trees. They entered the wood cautiously, but there was nothing to be heard but the singing of birds and the quick rustling of small creatures in the bushes, and the splashing of a stream not far away. The green twilight that closed in on them as they ventured farther into the wood was strange to Stiglaf. He was unused to the way the trees arched over and mingled their leaves and branches to shade the ground. But his feeling of strangeness was mild compared to Djamila's. The dark girl at his side, her eyes wide with amazement, clucked and clicked her tongue at the size of the trees, the lushness of the grass, and the green – everywhere the green.

They did not have to wait long to quench their thirst from the stream, nor to satisfy their hunger, for the bushes glowed with red and black berries, and the turf under the trees was scattered thick with nuts. In one clearing they sat down by silent agreement and, leaning against the trunk of a large tree, they ate their fill of crisp brown nuts and juicy fruit. Their meal done, Djamila lay back and slept, her head resting on her arm, while Stiglaf kept watch. The sun was now overhead. In an hour they must start out again.

Before long the tide would rise again in the bay and they must be aboard the ship again. He knew from the voyage that the days were shortening, and by night it would not be safe to stay on land. Who knew if the animals of the woods might not be dangerous? and if they offered no harm, then what of the men?

Regretfully he roused the sleeping girl, and they set off again. Stiglaf planned to move deeper into the wood, circling round so that their way would take them back to the beach and the ship. But they had not gone more than a hundred paces when the trees in front of them began to thin out and the light to increase. Stiglaf saw that they were coming near to a clearing or perhaps a forest track. Now they went more slowly, stepping with great care from tree to tree and bush to bush, looking ahead and around. Stiglaf stopped by a huge oak and signalled for Djamila to go more quietly. Before them, stretching far away through the trees, was a broad path, worn by men on foot and horseback and herds of cattle. Should they cross it or turn back?

Djamila caught her breath and dug her fingers into Stiglaf's shoulder. A man came striding down the path. He walked so close to the shelter of the trees that they had failed to see him in the distance. There was no time to slip back to the cover of the thicker part of the wood. Stiglaf hesitated, but Djamila pointed silently upward, then began to climb swiftly into the branches of the oak. Stiglaf followed her, slipping the spear he carried into the ferns at the foot of the tree. A thick covering of leaves only just starting to turn brown with autumn sheltered them from the ground. But by parting the branches they were able to see the track.

The man came nearer – a huge, barrel-shaped man, in dusty grey, with a broad red face and grey straggling locks of hair that hung down beneath a battered helmet. That and the sword at his side gave him the appearance of a wandering warrior, a masterless man. Stiglaf held his breath. Such men, driven from their own village for some crime, with every man's hand against him, could be treacherous and dangerous. But a second glance made him think again, for over his back the man carried a bag held by a broad strip of leather, a bag from which the hefts of tools projected. The wanderer was a craftsman, and as he came closer to their hiding-place, his grimy red face seemed amiable and cheerful. As he shambled along he opened his mouth wide, showing broken teeth, and he sang tunelessly.

Stiglaf smiled. The man was harmless. They had hidden from him for no reason. But even as he smiled, Djamila gripped his arm and pointed to the side. Her eyes, keen as a hawk's, had spotted something else. Some few paces behind the wanderer were two men, moving through the undergrowth with the skill and silence of snakes. They were helmeted and their swords were drawn. On they came, gaining on the older man, who went on his way in cheerful ignorance. When he had reached the tree they were almost on him. Stiglaf could hold back no longer.

"Look out, friend, behind you!" he shouted.

The craftsman did not turn his head, did not seem to hear. But his ambushers did and looked round wildly. Seeing nothing seemed to drive them to a desperate decision. They left their cover and leapt on their prey like wolves, snarling. But even as one sword caught him a crushing blow on the helmeted head, the victim, to Stiglaf's amazement, still did not turn. He staggered forward, arms flailing, trying to support himself against a tree-trunk. Another blow sent him down and the two of them were over him with swords raised, two-handed, to pin him to the ground.

Stiglaf turned to Djamila. Gesturing downward, he pointed to his own heels. Her keen mind ever alive, Djamila grasped his feet with both hands. Crouching an instant to secure his balance, Stiglaf launched his body forward through the branches. His outstretched hands sought a grip on a lower cross-branch some feet above the struggling men below, and as his fingers took hold, Stiglaf gave a great cry and Djamila let go his heels. Like a sling his body swung down and round in a great arc; his legs, held rigid, cut through the air, and at full stretch his feet, the wooden-shod crippled foot to the fore, struck one attacker a fearful blow behind the ear and below the protection of his helmet. Pitching forward, senseless, the man drove head

and shoulders into the chest of his accomplice, and together the two crashed to the turf in a tangle of arms and legs at the feet of their astonished victim.

His astonishment lasted no longer than it took him to draw breath. Nimbly, with a speed that ill-matched his grey hair and bulky body, the craftsman hurled himself at the marauders. One lay unconscious across the tree roots. The other, caring little for the fate of his companion, was on his feet and running for his life down the forest trail. His red face creased with laughter, the old man turned to Stiglaf who had dropped down to the ground and Djamila, who was sliding down the trunk of the oak tree. His eyes opened wide and his helmeted head wagged from side to side in happy bewilderment.

"Who are you, young folk, that drop from the trees like spirits to help me?" he asked in a roar.

To Stiglaf's astonishment, the man's speech, though strange in some of its sounds, was so close to the speech of the Skallings that he could grasp its meaning.

"Will you come with us to the shore?" he asked. "We will tell you who we are, but we must return to our ship before it floats away with the tide."

To his further amazement, the old man simply shook his head, and then raised both hands to his ears. And Stiglaf understood. He understood, too, why the man had allowed his attackers to creep so close upon him, and why the cries of warning had gone unheeded. The old man could not hear. Stiglaf held out his hand and grasped the great work-worn fingers in his. Then he pointed in the direction of the shore. To his surprise the old man suddenly grew angry.

"I'm not a dog to be drawn along the way," he bellowed. Taking Stiglaf by the shoulders he looked straight in the boy's face.

"Now speak and let me watch your lips. My ears are useless, but my old eyes are good. Let me see a man speak and I hear him as well."

Speaking slowly, Stiglaf repeated his words. For a moment the old man seemed puzzled, then he smiled and nodded. "Yes, I'll come with you. Why not? I am my own master and have nowhere better to go."

So they set out for the shore. And as they went, they heard the old man's story told in gusty roars and bellows. Years of deafness had caused him to shout rather than speak. His name was Guthlac, and all his life he had been a worker in metals in a place to the south. Years before, a quarrel had led to the death of a man, and Guthlac had been forced to leave his own village. He had wandered round in the hope that in time he might gain wealth enough to offer recompense to the family of the man who had died and thus be allowed to return to the place where he was born. His two attackers, followers of some lord who had cast them out of his band for crimes and drunkenness, had followed him from the last village where he had worked.

"Face to face, I would have been their match. For I not only make swords, but I can use them. But this curse of deafness betrayed me. And but for the fate that placed you in that tree above me, I would have died."

As Guthlac finished his tale, they came out from the woods on to the beach and saw that the tide had crept up the sand and was beginning to wash around the timbers of the ship. Guthlac stopped, a sudden wary look in his eyes.

"Such ships are not made in this land of the Angelcyn. By the prow I know that ship to come from the land of the Northmen, raiders and murderers."

His cheerful good spirits gone, old Guthlac drew back a pace and gripped his sword hilt.

"No farther. Is this some trap you have led me into with your talk of friendship? Come to our ship, you said. What do you want with Guthlac the Smith? Where are your crew men, where are they hidden? Who are you with your dark maid? Which land gave you birth, young man? Say or I'll go no farther. This smells of treachery."

Stiglaf stopped in his tracks and stared at Guthlac. The

old man dropped his bag on the ground and drew his sword:

"If you are men or spirits, speak. What are you? You drop from the trees like acorns. You sail on the sea in ships without crew. One of you is fair as day and one is dark as night. In all my days I have never seen the like of this."

Stiglaf dropped the spear and put out his hand to the old man. Looking straight into his eyes, he answered:

"We are not spirits, but wanderers like yourself. I am an exile from my own people, just as you are. This maid has wandered far from her own land. Be our friend. We are strangers here."

From behind him, Djamila croaked a warning. The tide had crept in and the boat had begun to rock and shift on its keel. Stiglaf waved Djamila on and the girl sped back to the sea and, splashing through the shallows, clambered over the side of the ship. Then Stiglaf turned back to the old man and said:

"Come, Guthlac, come with us. We cannot harm you."

Guthlac hesitated and Stiglaf turned to go to the ship, where Djamila was busy, clambering up the mast and securing the sail. He splashed into the water and had just swung himself over the gunwale when he heard a great roar.

"Here, young friend. Don't leave your spear. You'll have need of it yet."

There followed an enormous splashing, like a sea-lion diving. Then over the side of the ship tumbled the great leather bag, and after it came the huge red face of Guthlac the Smith, grey locks and helmet all askew. With a grunt the old man heaved himself up, and Djamila and Stiglaf rushed to help him aboard. Getting his breath back, the smith waddled to the stern and leaned his weight on the oar. Under his great strength the ship swung round. The prow turned to the open sea. From his place in the stern, the old man chuckled and shook his head to throw the wet locks of hair from his eyes.

"Now, where shall we sail?" he roared.

"Wherever we may find food and shelter," replied Stiglaf.

"I know a village to the south," said Guthlac, "where the people were once kind to me and I mended their ploughs. They will give shelter to wanderers if we come with good-will."

And so the ship set sail once more, bearing Stiglaf, Djamila and Guthlac to the south.

13

The moon rose and the water lapped softly under the prow as the three wanderers headed south. Djamila, curled up on the deck, her head resting against Stiglaf's leg, slept soundly. Stiglaf dozed and woke, unable to fall asleep completely, for his head was full with many thoughts. Only Guthlac, the tough old voyager, stayed fully awake, his arm slung over the stern oar as if it were the shoulder of an old friend. His keen eyes gazed into the darkness, watching the darker shadow of the coastline and the white leaping crests of the waves as they rose and fell. And, as they travelled, he talked, almost to himself.

"Wealdor, it is called, that village. A fine place. A man might tramp for a month through forest and mire before he came there, but in a fine little ship like this, we shall go handily. Old Guthlac shall eat the fat meat of the roast boar again and change stories with his old friends."

He bent quietly and ran his hand over the thick black curls on Djamila's head, as if to tell if they were real. The girl stirred in her sleep and Guthlac smiled and began to croon a song in his tuneless old voice. Stiglaf slept again, and when he woke, the old man was talking once more.

"Wealdor, it stands on a headland, between racing seas and a man must know what he's at to come in through the narrow gap that leads to the harbour. They keep watch there day and night for only by the sea can attackers get at them. It stands on the cliffs between sea and wood, and beyond the woods lie marshes and thickets, bog pools as deep as the earth, goblins and wood spirits. The land stands as it did before men came here, even before the people of the west, who were here before the Angelcyn came.

"The road to the north, which the conquerors from over the sea built, passes Wealdor by; it craftily loops round the marshes and leaves Wealdor alone. So no king or lord bothers Wealdor, nor do rovers and masterless men steal upon it without so much as a shout or a blast from a horn to warn good people. If a man comes there by land and does not know the secret way through the boglands, then he'll eat the bark of trees before he has a good meal again."

Stiglaf stretched himself. He asked:

"But what of raiders from the sea? Are these Wealdor people so strong that they do not fear the sea-rovers?"

"Lie down and sleep, lad. Aye, Wealdor was raided once, they say, by men in dragon ships, and they seized the chief's daughter. But that was many years ago, and the sea-rovers had a hard time of it."

"So was my mother carried away from her kin," said Stiglaf. "That could have been her village."

"Sleep, lad, think no more of it. Who knows how many years men have raided off these coasts, from east and north, as long as man has drawn sword or hoisted sail; or how many kin have been divided by death or stealing away. Few villages have had Wealdor's good fortune."

Stiglaf barely heard these last words as he slid away into sleep, and when he woke again the sun was up and Guthlac was craftily guiding the little ship into a small sheltered inlet, where the trees came close to the sand and all was quiet. When the ship was secure, Guthlac went into the woods and brought down three rabbits with stones from his sling, which he carried round his barrel waist like a belt. Then, taking from his pouch a tiny piece of charred cloth, an iron-hard pointed stick and small block of wood, he made fire in the shelter of the beached ship. For the first time since they had left the Skalling valley, Stiglaf and Djamila had the smell of roasting meat in their nostrils.

Before the sun had reached its full height, nothing was left of the three rabbits but a pile of bones and skin, and the three travellers were dozing contentedly in the ship's shadow. In the afternoon, as the tide rose, Guthlac roused them again and they made the ship ready for sailing. How easy it seemed to work the ship now that they had the strength and cunning of the wandering smith to aid them. And how strangely easy it was for all of them to speak to each other, though one was deaf and one was dumb and none of them had the same language. Such was Djamila's skill in signs that she and Guthlac had no need of words. When her thin dark fingers stretched and twirled their message, Guthlac would sometimes grasp their meaning before Stiglaf. What their senses lacked in speech and hearing they made up for with sharpness of eye and wits.

So, as they sailed to the south, day by day, the hours would often pass in silence. The autumn was advancing and the green gloom of the forests was changing to brown and red and gold, but the sky stayed clear and the sun shone and the following breeze was gentle and cool. They would sail by night, and by day seek out coves and inlets where no man lived and few came. There they would land, hunt game, gather herbs and berries and nuts. They would eat and sleep, Stiglaf and Guthlac would sing their own songs and tell tales of their own lands.

Slowly by the fireside, or on deck at night, Guthlac heard the whole story of Djamila and Stiglaf, of the Skallings, of Sven Fork-beard and his hero's death in the southern sea, of Red Arnulf and his ferocious son Torald. Stiglaf showed him the silver snake brooch his father had left him and the rune-carved comb. Guthlac scratched his grey head.

"I cannot tell runes, and what is written here is a mystery but one thing I know. The brooch is a sign of the people of the west and the runes are of the folk from the east, the Angelcyn.

"Your mother's kin must have been of both peoples. And this may be so, for it is true that there are places where those who came from the east, across the sea, did not drive out the people they found there, but lived side by side. Such a place was Wealdor. Long long ago, when Cerdic and his folk landed there, it is said, they could not overcome the people of Wealdor inside their stockade. Neither could the defenders drive them away. So it is said that Caerlin who commanded that place made a bond with Cerdic and the two peoples lived together. But, said Caerlin, they must promise one thing, that they would not send across the sea for more of their kind to join them. There was land enough for the two peoples, but for no more. And to this Cerdic loyally agreed, and the people from the east made their kin among those from the west.

"Or at least," said the old wanderer, "so I was told."

Stiglaf asked eagerly: "Do you think that my mother might have lived in such a place?"

The old man smiled. "Around these coasts are a thousand

inlets and harbours and more villages than a man may count, even a shepherd who knows how to count in great numbers. Don't hope too much, lad. From much hope comes much sorrow.

"Still," he added, when he saw the frown on Stiglaf's face, "in Wealdor all good men will find kin enough. It was so before and it will be so again."

Guthlac heaved up his vast body from the sands and began to rake out the fire.

"The tide's running, lad, and we've a way to go yet."

Djamila looked up and signalled with her fingers.

Guthlac pursed his lips.

"Seven days more we must sail, I think, before we can round the point and slide between the jagged rocks that guard Wealdor's harbour. But with fair winds and fair days it will pass soon enough. I have, so I believe, passed three-score summers in my time, and who knows how many days that is. And where have they gone? Be of good heart and we shall soon come to Wealdor." And with that Guthlac led the way through the shallows to the waiting ship.

As the days passed the sun shone, the woods yielded good food, and the night brought fresh breezes and everything seemed in their favour. So the travellers, as they drew towards their journey's end, became careless. One day, at noon, after they had eaten, they forgot to set a watch. Or perhaps one who had agreed to keep watch nodded off to sleep. But suddenly Djamila, whose ears were sharpest, caught the faint tremor of feet. Cautiously, she raised her head, then shook Stiglaf. He bent his head to the ground and listened. Without a doubt, someone was coming. It was a confused sound that meant perhaps one, perhaps two men. Quickly they roused Guthlac, and the old warrior, still grunting and rubbing his eyes, motioned them to hide behind the prow of the ship. The tide was still out and there was no chance to launch and escape.

"Let us hope it is no more than two. We three may handle two, as we did in the woods when you saved my life," he growled.

They waited in the shadow of the prow. The moments passed slowly in silence and then, through the trees, came a strange but pleasant sound. Someone was singing as he walked and played to himself on a stringed instrument whose notes floated light but clear through the trees. The three looked at one another in amazement. Who could be wandering the shore-line, singing in this way? Then, out of the shelter of the trees came a lone figure, in a long dark cloak, and walking in the strangest manner. As he came nearer, they saw that his hair was close-cropped.

"If he be a monk," said Stiglaf, "those are not the holy psalms he is singing. That last song more fits an alehouse. His monastery must be the strangest in all the land."

The "monk" came slowly closer. He would lift the staff he carried and swing it in front of him in wide sweeps. Then he would tuck the staff under his arm, take up his harp again, and play and sing, but walking in a wandering way until he set his course right again by swinging his stick. Now he was clear of the trees and on the beach, his sandals scuffing on the sand and shells. He came on, cheerfully singing.

Stiglaf gasped. "Either he is a man of no fear at all or he is drunk."

"True, lad," replied Guthlac. "What monk could walk

towards a dragon-prowed ship, even one so small as ours, without fear, unless he were mad or drunk?"

But Djamila shook her head violently, pulled at their sleeves and pointed quickly to her own eyes.

"By Odin, yes!" roared Guthlac, his surprised voice carrying half across the beach. "The monk is blind. He does not see us."

The monk stopped in his swaying walk, some twenty paces away.

"But I hear you," he called. "Tell me, are you friends and true believers?"

"What does he say?" growled Guthlac. "I cannot see his lips at this distance."

Stiglaf repeated the monk's words and Guthlac suddenly roared with laughter.

"We be true believers all, but all with our own gods. We have all the gods on earth in our little band. And what of you?"

The monk hesitated. "Your voice is kind, if your words are rough, friend. I am a wandering monk, late of Alcuin's company. I believe in the one true God."

Stiglaf stood up and advanced from the shadow of the ship. He spoke quietly so as not to alarm the blind man.

"Good friend. Have no fear. We would not harm you, a wanderer like ourselves and one whom the gods have tried. We are but three, a lame lad, a dumb maid, and a deaf old man."

The monk smiled and came forward. "Then have you room in your band for one who cannot see a step before him, who has not seen the light of day, the sky, the trees, or the sea for many years?"

"Gladly," answered Stiglaf, and held out his hands

towards the monk, who took them after a moment's searching in the air. Now that they were close, Stiglaf saw that the monk was only a few years older than he and that beneath the cropped head was a round freckled face and hazel eyes. "What is your name?"

"My name is Aelwyn. For ten years I was a brother in a monastery far to the north. But now I am on my way home to live with my own people."

"And where is home?" asked Guthlac, who had come with Djamila to stand directly behind Stiglaf's shoulder.

"Home is the fairest village in this land and the kindest. Home is Wealdor."

Guthlac let out a great roar of delighted laughter. "Why, friend, this is fate. For we three are bound for Wealdor."

The monk's face was puzzled. "How can that be? You do not speak as men of Wealdor do. You are strangers."

"No," replied Guthlac. "I am no man of Wealdor, but neither am I a stranger. I have visited and lived there three times in ten years, while you were away on your monk's business. And this young lad, who comes from the land of the Northmen, and the maid who comes from the strange lands below the southern sea, are wanderers on the earth. I have told them they will find a welcome in Wealdor."

"Why, that is true," said Aelwyn. "And that is why I am going home. For my heart has been a stranger all these years and I longed to be again on the cliffs of Wealdor."

"Then come in our ship," said Stiglaf. "It will carry you faster than your legs."

Aelwyn frowned. "Your ship? But you said there were only three of you."

"So there are," laughed Guthlac, "but it is a small ship,

having been made in the first place for only one man and he not alive and not wanting much room. There is room, though, for one more in the crew."

"But I fear that I am no crew man. I know nothing of ships," said the monk.

"Why," said Stiglaf, "when you can sing as sweetly and cheerfully as you do, we shall ask for no more. Come, the tide is running. We have food on board. Djamila will give you something to eat and she will teach you the language of signs we use."

"What use are signs to me," asked the monk, "if I cannot see?"

Djamila answered him by taking his hand in her long fingers and tracing on his palm the outline of a ship and over it a sign. Stiglaf, looking over her shoulder, said: "That means welcome to our craft."

Aelwyn smiled: "At last, to have found true friendship among heathens, after so many years' cold comfort among men of God."

Guthlac helped, or rather lifted, the young monk over the side of the ship. "You are now among men of gods, not men of God. We are men, and maid, of every god you can dream of. But tell us, Aelwyn of Wealdor, follower of Alcuin, why did you leave your holy place after so many years?"

The monk rested his back against the ship's timbers, while the three began to tend the sail and man the stern oar and the ship began to draw away from the shore. He raised his wide-mouthed, freckled face to the sea breeze and breathed deeply.

"In the house of the Lord I learnt to sing the psalms and the brothers had me play for them. They taught me to write the word of God in fine sheepskin scrolls and to carve runes on holy crosses until my sight failed me. So the monks would have me make tunes for the psalms. But I could not unlearn the songs I sang as a boy in Wealdor, the songs I heard from the women as they worked and the shepherds by their sheep, songs and riddles of all manner of earthly things. The abbot and the brothers reasoned with me, but I could not banish those tunes and words from my mind – even when the great Alcuin himself sent word.

"Then the abbot put into my mind the thought that I should take the old tunes I knew and set the holy words of the psalms to them. Which pleased the brothers, for though the one true God has the best words, the old gods have the best tunes."

Guthlac laughed at this and shouted a snatch of a drinking song from his place at the stern oar.

Aelwyn nodded.

"Such a song was my undoing. For in the church, while I led the singing, the holy words would slip from my mind and in their place would come words of love and praise of beer."

"So they cast you out?" asked Stiglaf.

"No, I went in shame, to wander back to my home," the monk replied.

"Ha, what of it?" said Guthlac. "Such was your fate. The wind blows. The sailor may trim his sail and tack here or there, but the wind will bring him home or cast him on the rocks."

"Not so," answered Aelwyn sharply, his pleasant freckled face suddenly grim. "A man does not yield to blind fate. He learns to know the way of the Lord and what the Lord wishes him to do."

Stiglaf interrupted: "What do you say to this, then, Aelwyn? Before I was born, my father went to Unna, old woman of the hills, and she prophesied to him that his son would be a cripple among cripples. Well, is that not my fate and has it not come to pass? Here we are together, each of us a cripple in the eyes of our fellow-men. Such is fate." And he told Aelwyn briefly the story of his travels.

Guthlac nodded. "Indeed. Such is fate and there is no going against it. One must live it out as best one may."

"No, not," cried Aelwyn. "See, there is nothing blind about the way of Stiglaf's life. At each turn he had to choose. Should he protect the girl Djamila? Should he rescue Guthlac in the woods? Should he aid a blind wanderer who did not believe in his gods? He has been guided in his choice by a providence that watches over us."

"And did this providence also set those wolves upon me in the woods? And did it set Stiglaf's own kin to harry and hound him and cast this young girl to the flames? If so, then it is wicked and not good," growled Guthlac.

Aelwyn was about to reply when Stiglaf intervened.

"Please, Aelwyn. Sing us a song and let us not quarrel just when we have become friends."

Aelwyn smiled. "Many years of disputing with my brothers have given me a liking for it. No, it's better to sing. Better still, I will sing you a riddle and you shall all seek the answer."

"Then be sure to look into my face when you sing, brother," said Guthlac, "or I shall not know your question."

Aelwyn took up his harp and began to sing:

"What has no eyes but sees all that passes?
What hears no evil but knows good?

What has no tongue but says all that is needful?
What cannot run but is everywhere?"

He paused, and the others shook their heads. He laughed and sang:

"*Friendship – the love of true friends.*"

Then he struck the strings again and Stiglaf and Guthlac joined in, while Djamila, smiling, beat time with her hand, and the ship sailed on to the south, towards Wealdor.

14

By the next day, Aelwyn was already an experienced and welcome member of the band. With his knowledge of runes and writings, he was able to learn swiftly the meaning of Djamila's signs, and with the others to guide him, he soon found his way around the ship without the aid of his staff. Like the others, too, he grew more cheerful as the ship sailed on under the blue, cloud-flecked skies, closer and closer to Wealdor.

On the last day of the voyage the four companions rested on the beach after their midday meal, content and quiet, speaking little. Stiglaf remembered that in the pouch at his belt lay the little comb carved with runes, and the strange, snake brooch which had belonged to his mother. Now he took them out and shyly asked Aelwyn:

"You are skilled in the reading of runes. Can you tell me what is the meaning of this?"

Aelwyn took up the carved comb and ran his fingers lightly over the ridges and hollows of the carving. For a moment he smiled and then he looked puzzled.

"It says, 'All the teeth of the comb are of the same length,' which means that all men are as good as one another. But how did you come by this?"

"It belonged to my mother, who came from these islands."

"It is strange," said Aelwyn, "for I have heard this saying among the older women in Wealdor. And this brooch with its figure of the snake – in the old belief of the people of the west it means life everlasting. And again, among the old people of Wealdor, I have seen such ornaments."

He sat for a while in silence. Then he turned to Stiglaf and said:

"What was your mother's name?"

"Deira," replied Stiglaf.

Aelwyn leapt to his feet, scattering the ash of the fire. "Deira? That cannot be!"

Stiglaf's heart beat wildly. "What do you mean?"

"Yes, speak, Aelwyn," roared Guthlac. "What mystery is in your head?"

Aelwyn sank down again on the ground and stared out towards the sea. The others looked at him in wonder as he began to speak.

"In the years before I was born – and thus I only know what my mother told me – Wealdor endured a raid by Northmen, the most terrible raid it had known. Only the fiercest and most desperate sea-rovers could come through the narrow straits between the Wealdor cliffs. Only the boldest and most courageous could climb the cliff path from the sea. Only the strongest could storm the stockade that guards the homes of Wealdor, or breach the great timbers of the meet-hall, where the Wealdor men could make a last fighting stand.

"But in this year of which I tell you came just such a band of raiders. They came in two ships; they forced the narrow passage by night, a feat of reckless daring. Rowing with muffled oars, they slipped past the guards and climbed the narrow path like goats in the early dawn. Before the men of Wealdor could leap to their weapons, they had reached the stockade.

"But a band of men under Cerdic, of the line of Cerdic, greatest man of Wealdor, resisted them at the gate, while Cyntha, wife of Cerdic, and her women drove away the cattle into the woods and marshes and hid themselves where no stranger could find them. Cerdic's men, hard-pressed, drew back into the meet-hall and withstood all assaults. It seemed that the attack had failed. What was more, the raiders were in peril themselves.

"They had little food, counting on feasting at the tables of Wealdor, which had been swept bare by the women in their flight. And so closely did the Wealdor people keep watch that the raiders did not dare try to retreat for fear they might be slaughtered before they could reach their ships in the harbour below. But the raiders had one piece of good fortune. They had seized a young woman, kin to Cerdic, as she sought to bring a message from the people in the woods. They held her as hostage and tried to make terms with the men of Wealdor, to give them food and let them return in peace to their ships. The men of Wealdor, that is, the oldest and wisest, wanted to accept these terms. They knew that the raiders would not hasten to attack Wealdor again and they knew that further fighting meant more bloodshed. But the younger men spurned the terms, seeking revenge for those killed. Cerdic denied them revenge. He said it was a two-edged sword, cutting the man who held it. He said that the raiders should be allowed to leave silently in the night, so that no man might see them going, if they would give back the young woman they held as hostage.

"But in the night a band of young Wealdor men, breaking the word given by Cerdic, tried to encircle and attack the raiders. There might have been a terrible killing but for the hostage. She got word of the treachery and warned the raiders, who slipped away in good time. Just as they boarded the ship and the young woman watched from the shore, several young warriors ran down the cliff path and saw all. In their rage at being cheated, they made to kill the young woman there and then. But, so the story goes, a great black-bearded raider leapt from his ship and with whirling axe scattered the young men and carried off the woman into the darkness."

Stiglaf could hardly hold his excitement.

"What was her name, Aelwyn, what was her name?"

The monk replied: "Her name was Deira, of the line of Cerdic."

Stiglaf leapt up, throwing his arms wide.

"Then I am sure that was my mother and the raider who rescued her from her own kin, and carried her off, was Sven Fork-beard, my own father."

"No, that cannot be, surely!" cried Guthlac.

"She gave this brooch and this rune-carved comb to my father and made him promise that he would raid no more. This promise he kept for many years, until the last raid to the southern sea, when he was killed," said Stiglaf.

"Then, if that be true," said Aelwyn, "you have kin in Wealdor."

"Aye," put in the shrewd Guthlac, "but what of the kin of the young men who sought to kill his mother and were themselves killed by the black raider, his father?"

"You need have no fear of them," answered Aelwyn, "for when the people of Wealdor heard what had happened, the families of the young men cried shame on their evil recklessness and word-breaking."

Aelwyn stood up and took Stiglaf's arm. "Come, friends, let us get to sea and not lose a moment until we sail into harbour in Wealdor. There will be a welcome for all wanderers, but for the son of Deira of the line of Cerdic, there will be a double welcome."

The others needed no urging and swiftly boarded the ship. Aelwyn struck up a tune on his harp, Guthlac worked the ship out to sea, and the wind blew more strongly. The waves foamed against the prow and the ship sped southward. That night there was little sleep for any on board, and the dawn found Stiglaf and Djamila in the prow eagerly searching the horizon. Behind them, Aelwyn asked:

"Do you see tall white cliffs?"

"Yes!" they cried.

"Do you see a great rock standing alone like a giant bathing his feet in the waves?"

"Yes."

"Then, Guthlac, we must head straight for that rock."

"Straight for the rock?" demanded Guthlac.

"Aye, straight for the rock and through the Giant's Legs, as the folk of Wealdor say, for that is the entrance to the harbour." Aelwyn turned to Stiglaf. "Your father was a bold and skilful sailor to have forced the passage."

Now Guthlac leaned on the sweep, the waves boiled and foamed around the stern and lashed and pounded at the foot of the cliffs ahead. But guided by Aelwyn, whose keen ear caught the roar of water on the rocks on either side,

Guthlac steered the ship through the narrow channel. Like a deer leaping, the little craft cleared the breakers and shot into the calm water of the harbour, ringed with rock and golden sand, while all above them towered the shining white cliffs.

"Wealdor," cried Stiglaf.

"Wealdor!" roared Guthlac.

Djamila clapped her dark hands and danced on the deck, her long legs making the red tunic leap.

"Stay," said Aelwyn. "Is there a watcher on the cliffs?"

Stiglaf scanned the white wall.

"No, there are small boats on the beach. I see a dog running off across the sand, but I see no man, woman nor child."

"Look again," commanded Aelwyn, with more force.

They looked, and again Stiglaf answered: "No, I see no one."

Aelwyn's face grew dark. "Then we must go with care."

"Maybe," said Guthlac, "the sight of the dragon prow has scared all folks from the shore."

"The men of Wealdor," answered Aelwyn firmly, "are no cowards. A single ship would not drive them from the cliffs. Indeed, I thought there might be a whole band of armed men on the lookout."

"Then we must go and see what's amiss," said Guthlac cheerfully, slapping the monk on the shoulder. "Maybe they are all at their breakfast," he added, licking his lips. "And we shall shortly join them."

But Aelwyn's anxious look did not go.

"Let me lead the way," he said. "I know the cliff path so well I need no guide. And if the Wealdor folk are alarmed, they will know me and be reassured."

"Yes," said Stiglaf, "but we shall come close behind you, for fear there is some mischief."

They left the ship cautiously, the blind monk in the lead tapping with his staff on the rocks and stones of the beach As they climbed the narrow twisting path, Stiglaf pictured in his mind his father and the Skalling warriors climbing this very cliff, their feet gripping these same dents in the hard-packed ground. He pictured his mother waiting on the beach for the onslaught of the maddened young men of Wealdor, and his father leaping from the prow to rescue her from her own people. Inside him sadness and excitement tangled together.

Suddenly the cliff path ended and they were on the broad turf-covered top, the sea wind blustering about them. In front lay endless green stretches of wild wood reaching to the farther skyline. And before the forest, proud and firm, stood the logged stockade, the turfed roofs of Wealdor. Aelwyn gripped him by the arm.

"Is there smoke from the rooftops?"

"No," said Stiglaf. "Not a wisp."

"Is the great gate shut?"

"No, it lies wide open."

The four travellers advanced slowly, bewilderment and anxiety growing with every step. The dog they had seen on the beach suddenly appeared in front of them, sniffed the air and ran away in front, its tail held between its legs. Nothing else was stirring as they reached the stockade and looked inside. Stiglaf saw several score dwellings arranged in a circle around a great space, over which loomed a great fire hall, bigger even than the great hall of the Skallings.

"Aelwyn. The meet-hall has no roof. The rafters are black and open to the sky."

Aelwyn began frantically to call out the names of people that he knew. His voice bounced back from the trees. In the centre of the space before the hall, a long cooking trench was dug in the soil. Beside it lay cauldrons, gourds, pots and cooking tools. In the trench the remains of a fire still smouldered, and some of the dishes contained food. Guthlac bent and picked up one of the bowls, fingering the food in it. He turned to Stiglaf.

"Here is something strange. Folk at their morning meal, many folk. But now all gone. We must tread warily. Do you and Aelwyn search every house and the maid, whose eyes are sharp, and I will go round the stockade and search the cattle pens."

Stiglaf nodded. From house to house he wandered with Aelwyn, who called out the names of people he knew.

But only hens and chicks ran out squawking and chirping, and a fat sow with her litter lumbered out of their way. The village was empty. Not a man, woman or child was to be found. And shortly Guthlac and Djamila came back with the same tale.

Some great misfortune had struck the happy village of Wealdor. But what had become of her people?

15

Aelwyn sank down on the ground and put his head on his folded arms. His shoulders shook with his weeping. Guthlac slowly and clumsily lowered his great bulk to kneel beside the young man and put an arm round his shoulders.

"Have courage, lad. All's not lost. Your folk have not long left this place. They cannot be far away, and for sure your god or my gods or Djamila's god will look after them."

Aelwyn turned up a tear-stained face.

"You mock me, Guthlac, though you do it kindly."

Guthlac's forehead creased.

"I, mock? Not I. Listen. I have seen much in my three-score years. Never anything like this. I have seen villages put to the sword and plundered, but they were not like this. Plunderers do not leave houses untouched. Nor do they carry away the dead they have robbed of life, nor those they have maimed. If Wealdor has been raided, where are the dead and dying, where are the marks of plunder? The only ashes are here in the cooking fire."

"What of the meet-hall? That is burnt," said Stiglaf.

"True, lad. But it was not burnt to-day, nor yesterday, nor even last year. Why, there is not even the whiff of burning. The people are gone, as if they were spirited away. There is magic at work here."

"That is superstition," said Aelwyn, brushing his sleeve across his face.

"You may call it what you will. But your holy books will never give an answer to marvels like this," retorted Guthlac. "See," he went on. "We must return to our vessel, for our own safety, bearing with us, for I am sure no one will say nay, some of this tasty food which it would be wrong to leave uneaten. There we shall wait awhile and see what happens. Soon we shall have our answer."

Stiglaf nodded. The old campaigner knew best. The four gathered together some scraps of food and, watched only by the dog which still slunk around the homes, and the sow with her young, they made their way out of the stockade and to the cliffs. Back on the beach by their ship, they ate, even Aelwyn ate a little, and then Guthlac said calmly:

"I shall sleep an hour. You, Stiglaf, may keep watch with Aelwyn for I doubt he will sleep. Then we may talk again of what we must do. Maybe the same spirit that carried away the Wealdor folk will bring them back," and with that, Guthlac leaned his broad back against a sloping rock and was soon snoring gustily. Djamila, too, lay down, though she could not sleep. With Stiglaf she watched Aelwyn as the young monk wandered to and fro along the shore. An hour passed slowly and Guthlac, true to his word, even in sleep, slowly began to stir his great body. Aelwyn returned from his pacing to and fro and sat down.

Suddenly Djamila held up her finger and leaned her head on one side. Her eyebrows rose until they almost vanished in her black hair. Then she laid her fingers on Stiglaf's wrist and traced a sign on them.

Stiglaf's eyes widened.

"An ox?"

She nodded.

Now Stiglaf listened too, and when Aelwyn demanded to know what he was about, signalled for him to be quiet. Djamila was right. Somewhere, not far away, an ox was lowing, faint but clear. But where was it? There had been no cattle in the stockade, nor in the woods around. And cattle lowing in the woods could not be heard down here on the beach.

Guthlac grunted, snorted and awoke. He stared comically at the three young people, who listened so intently, their heads to one side.

"Ah, you hear spirit-songs," he grinned.

"We hear oxen and they are flesh and blood," replied Stiglaf.

Aelwyn leapt to his feet, striking his head, and began to stride across the sand, swinging his staff before him. The others, amazed, followed as he headed towards the cliffs.

Stiglaf caught up with him: "What is it, Aelwyn?"

"The caves," replied the monk.

"Caves? There are no caves," said Stiglaf.

"There are caves – a narrow opening right in face of the Giant's rock."

"No," insisted Stiglaf. "There are only trees and bushes in the face of the cliff."

By now the other two had caught up with them and the four halted some dozen paces from the clump of small trees and bushes that grew out of fissures in the face of the cliff. Aelwyn hesitated a moment and then went forward, followed by the others. When he reached the bushes he began to pull at them, but they stayed firmly rooted in the soil. He shook his head in bewilderment, but then, quite clearly, as if it sounded from the heart of the rock, came the lowing of an ox. Guthlac lumbered back to the ship and returned, panting, with a short-handled axe from his bag. A few sharp strokes and the first bushes were cut free or pulled aside. The three saw to their astonishment not the white of the cliff but the blackness of a tunnel running into it.

"Caves," said Stiglaf.

"Aye, caves. As I said," replied the monk. "I remember them from a boy. A long narrow opening, leading to a great cavern under the earth. Come."

And with that, sure-footed as if he had never been blind, Aelwyn pushed his way past the bush-screen and vanished inside the cliff.

The other three followed, stumbling and slipping behind his hastening footsteps. At first all was pitch-black around them, but soon they saw light ahead. Again came the sound of lowing, but now louder and unmistakable, and more quietly the sound of shuffling feet, animals or men, then more distinctly the whispering sound that could only come from the lips of men or women. The passage ended abruptly, falling away into a huge cave whose ceiling could not be seen in the gloom.

But in the middle of the cavern, lit by the glow of half a dozen torches stuck into holes in the face of the chalk, was a sight that brought gasps of amazement from the three behind Aelwyn. The cavern was packed until hardly a foot of space was left to stand, with cattle – cows, goats, sheep and horses. The air was thick with their smell. And beyond them, in the darker limits of the cave, were people, perhaps a score or more, and with them children, whose subdued sobbing rose every now and then, only to be silenced by their elders.

Aelwyn stepped forward into the light and, without warning, like a deadly shadow, a spear thrown from behind the cattle flew between Stiglaf and him, and thudded deep into the chalk behind them. It passed so close that Stiglaf felt its whisper in his ear.

"Back," he called to Aelwyn, but the blind monk went on.

"Good people of Wealdor," he cried, his voice trembling, not with fear but with joy. "Have no fear. It is Aelwyn, son of Wulfstan, Aelwyn the monk and his three true friends. His friends are yours. They will not harm you."

In the darkness a woman called the monk's name, but another voice intervened, a young voice, that of a boy, but strong and unafraid.

"If you are truly Aelwyn, son of Wulfstan, come forward and let us see your face. But bid your companions stay back. We will have no treachery."

Aelwyn stepped forward blindly amid the cattle, running his hand over their great backs, rubbing their noses as he moved confidently among them. As he passed out of the other side of the herd, he was seized on, and there was the muffled sound of embracing and weeping and more talking. Then Aelwyn turned and called across the cavern.

"Come, Djamila, Guthlac, Stiglaf. Come and greet my people. But take care to come round by the side of the cave. The long-horned cattle of Wealdor are fierce to those they do not know."

In a moment the three companions found themselves in the middle of an excited crowd of people who stared at them, while the children shyly touched them.

The voice of Guthlac boomed out:

"But what has come to pass with Wealdor? Are there no warriors? I see none but old men, women and children."

Then he turned to the boy who had spoken earlier and said: "Lad, I ask pardon when I speak of children. I see that you bear yourself like a man, yet if my old eyes see right, you are no more than twelve years."

"It is true," replied the lad. "But when Wealdor has no men, then children must become men in their place. I am Cerdic, son of Brydo of the line of Cerdic. Say who you are?"

"I am Guthlac, a wanderer and a smith, and a man known to people in Wealdor. I have been guest in your homes before and have done work for warrior and farmer."

"I am Stiglaf, son of Sven . . ."

"A Northman," broke in the lad, his voice hostile.

"Peace, Cerdic," said Aelwyn. "Stiglaf is our friend and he is more. He is your kin and the kin of others in Wealdor." The monk raised his voice until it echoed in the roof of the cavern. "This is Stiglaf, son of Sven and son of Deira of the line of Cerdic."

At his words there was a sudden silence. From among the crowd a tall woman, upright and firm of features, stepped forward and took a torch from the wall. She held it close to Stiglaf's face while she looked closely at him.

"If I had another sign, I could believe it. Deira was my cousin."

Stiglaf burrowed in his pouch and held up in the light of the torch the silver brooch and the carved comb. The woman seized them, looked them over keenly, then pressed them back into Stiglaf's hand. "Greetings, son of Deira. I am Hilde, mother of Cerdic." She turned to the

Wealdor folk who gathered round. "This is a good sign for us. We lost Deira through the headstrong foolishness of our young warriors. Now that they are gone from us, Deira's son has come to us." The crowd murmured and pressed round Stiglaf, peering at his face, the older women touching his long, fair hair. Then Cerdic spoke.

"Greetings, Stiglaf. You must know the story of Deira. But have no fear of blood feud. Those young men your father fought with here on the beach at Wealdor, before you or I were born, are no longer with us. They are dead or gone, every one. Wealdor has no warriors, only women and old men, and boys and girls."

"Why," said Guthlac from behind Stiglaf's shoulder, "while Wealdor has boys like you, it has no need of men. But say, Cerdic, son of Brydo, why do the people of Wealdor, who have the fairest village in the land, live like goblins in the dark?"

"We saw a ship with a dragon prow in the sea, heading for our cliffs. And since these days we are not able to resist, we took flight. We planned to hide until the raiders grew tired of searching and sailed away."

"Then set your heart at rest," said Guthlac. "That was our ship. Aelwyn guided us safely through the Giant's Legs. And since it is our ship, it is also yours. For what we have shall be yours and we will gladly help you, just as Wealdor people helped me in the past."

"But say," said Aelwyn. "How did people and cattle come into these caves? For the outer entrance is blocked with bushes, whose roots are fast in the earth."

"Last year," answered Cerdic, "the ground gave way in the woods above, and showed us a passage into the earth, a tunnel down into this cavern. We left the bushes and trees to grow both to seaward and to landward, but left room above for man and beast to pass in single file down into the caves in time of danger. When our lookouts give warning we do not wait, but hide ourselves with all our best cattle." He shrugged. "So we live and shall live for another five, maybe ten years until the young boys grow tall and strong enough to take the warriors' place."

While he was speaking, Hilde gave directions to the people around them, and with a great shouting, bleating and lowing, they began to drive the herd before them through the farther side of the cavern and up a gentle slope lit by torches. It was a full hour before the last beast and human had found their way out of the stench-filled air of the hideout and into the fresh air of the autumn forest. But within another hour, the smoke was rising from the homes of Wealdor, the fire was glowing in the cooking trench before the high meet-hall with its blackened burnt-out roof, and a meal was being prepared. Stiglaf and Djamila sat amid the curious eyes of busy women and playing children, while Aelwyn wandered from one group to another asking after this friend and that. Guthlac tore himself away from the roasting meat to pace round the stockade and survey the approach from the seaward with the eye of a veteran. He came back to find the others sitting down to eat. He placed himself between Stiglaf and Cerdic, with a huge arm round each lad's shoulder.

"A word from an old warrior. This place may be stormed at any time by a handful of desperate men creeping out of the forests or crawling up the cliff. You will never be safe, Cerdic, I fear."

The lad nodded grimly. "I know, but what can we do?"

The old smith plucked up a leg of pork and chewed on it with relish for a while.

"The stockade cannot be defended. But the meet-hall might be. If it were rebuilt, it would hold all the people who are now in Wealdor. It would be wisdom indeed to move all families within the hall when winter comes, for the sake of warmth and good fellowship. Then Aelwyn might sing and I might tell stories and we might pass the dark days merrily."

"But how can we rebuild the meet-hall?" asked Cerdic.

The old smith finished his bone and rubbed his belly with a grin. "Counting the biggest of the boys and your old men, some of whom still have strength, though," he added with a sly look round, "they have grown used to sitting on their haunches talking of the old days. Counting them and the women, those who can be spared from tending the beasts and cooking, we shall have nearly a score of willing pairs of hands. And, with such a band, I, Guthlac the Smith, can build a meet-hall twice as high as this."

At his words, there was a general shout of agreement around the cooking-place.

Cerdic leapt up and cried: "Let it be so. To-morrow we shall begin. Wealdor shall rise again."

16

The next day the rebuilding of the great meet-hall began. The harvest was nearly over, and soon almost everyone who had strength to lift and carry, to cut and shape wood, to prepare bolts and thongs, was at work, from first light to sunset. Through all the confusion waddled the barrel-like figure of Guthlac, urging, commanding, advising, his face red and sweating, his roaring voice raising the birds in the treetops. He never listened to those who contradicted him; in fact, he never heard them, though no one could help but hear him. He would give heed only to Djamila, for whose forethought and cunning he had great respect. It was Djamila who thought of having two false dragon prows shaped out of wood, which were then bolted on to the prow of the little ship in which they had arrived. This was then moored securely near the narrow entrance to the harbour. Thus from the sea it seemed that three longships were in the harbour, enough to make any sea-raider pause. From the landward side, the Wealdor people felt more secure as winter drew on, for they were sure that the marshes beyond the woods were impassable during the months of rain, snow and ice.

Before winter set in, then, the great hall was roofed once more and the inside furnished, the women preparing great curtains of cow hide to divide eating and sleeping quarters. As the first snowflakes began to drift down from grey November skies, the great hall was complete. The cattle were herded into their pens and the doors to each of the family homes made fast. Then with great feasting and much laughter, and new songs from Aelwyn, the people drew back into their winter stronghold. At the end of each short winter day the families hurried into the safe, firelit hall, and the outer door was barred.

In the winter evenings all sat together round the long tables, like "teeth in a comb", as Guthlac put it. And Stiglaf and his friends learned the full story of Wealdor's fall from good fortune. It was finally told them by Hilde, Cerdic's mother. She spoke unwillingly, for the story was an unhappy one, and the newcomers hesitated to seek an answer to the question – where had the warriors gone? But at last Hilde told them the story.

"After your mother, Stiglaf, was taken by the raiders from the north, there was bad feeling among the Wealdor folk, and while this lasted things did not go well. But one day a wandering monk came to us through the woods, a follower of Alcuin, teaching the belief of his god, which he said was Lord over all things, man or beast. Now, in Wealdor, men have always prayed within their own households, whether it be to Odin or Tiw the Thunderer or even older gods. No man seeks to know what another does. But this monk, who was a good man, humble and poor, taught that there must be no bitter feeling among God's creatures, that past differences should be forgotten, and that no blood feud should be allowed to cause enmity. This was a welcome teaching to Cerdic, who had lost his daughter because of men's wish for revenge. So the monk was allowed to stay with us for two summers and one winter, and when he went back to his own people he left many behind who believed in his god. But of this we thought no more, save Wulfstan, who was so taken with the new beliefs that he allowed his son Aelwyn to travel north to the followers of Alcuin and become one of them.

"But after some years another came, an abbot with his monks, and lived among us for a while, a proud man and haughty, more like a soldier than a priest. Cunningly he talked to our young men, telling them of cruelties done to followers of his god in lands to the north. When he went away a score of our young men followed him. Ten died in battles far away, ten came home to sow discontent among the warriors that remained. While he lived, Cerdic could keep this talk in check, but when he died, Brydo, my husband, who should have followed Cerdic in keeping peace among the Wealdor folk, joined with those warriors who had returned in stirring up the young men.

"Then one autumn the abbot returned to Wealdor. This time an armed chief came with him, a man with a face so cruel I shall never forget its black wickedness. They told us that the Christian lord to the north was menaced by the heathen lord to the west. What did these things mean to us? Christian, heathen, to us it was an old and evil game, one man against another. But the warriors, led by Brydo, were on fire to go. I think the long years of idleness made them ready to listen to any madness. And the abbot talked so cleverly."

Hilde sighed. "They marched away, three-score men – some mere youths, some fathers of families – marched to the west before the snows fell. And they never returned. And that is why Wealdor is in this unhappy state."

Stiglaf nodded, and in his turn told the story of the Skallings and the pledge that Sven Fork-beard had made to Deira his wife, a pledge broken with his death on the shores of the southern sea.

Hilde smiled. "Fate, then, is not so blind. Its winds have brought the son of Deira to our shores, with true companions to help the people of Wealdor. This winter we shall feel safe for the first time since our men went away."

The winter passed and spring came on. The ditches in the woods ran with melted snow and warmer winds blew from the south. The herds were let loose from their winter pens and the long-horned cattle, fierce with hunger, charged madly out into the woodland meadows.

And, with the spring, a strange thing happened. Six ragged, starving men, who had lurked in the woods and marshes most of the winter – deserters or stragglers from a fighting force on the march – staggered through the opening of the stockade one day. Two of them were recognised and welcomed with joy by the Wealdor folk – two brothers Oswy and Ecfrith. They and their four companions, survivors of a disastrous battle to the west, had struggled back, their one hope of life being to reach Wealdor.

For seven days the six men were treated like princes, their strength restored with good food, their clothes cleaned and repaired by the women. Each night in the meet-hall they drank and sang with great spirit, though Guthlac frowned at their boasting. But after the seven days had passed the returned warriors, now fully recovered, ceased to be the centre of care and admiration. The Wealdor folk went about their business, tending the herds, planting and sowing, repairing buildings and cattle pens, seeing to the small boats on the beach. The work went on around them, but the six, lounging at their table in the great hall, made no move to help. They sat idly polishing buckles and sword hilts, drinking or talking among themselves. Cerdic came to Stiglaf and asked his advice. Stiglaf called Aelwyn, Djamila and Guthlac to him, and the five talked over what must be done. Guthlac was brief: "A man that will not work, neither shall he eat. We are not rich enough for idlers."

That night in the hall, no food was laid at the end of the great table, where the six warriors sat. For a while they waited, while all around them ate and drank, then the biggest of them, a lean black-bearded man, strode up to Cerdic and demanded roughly:

"Why is no place set for us?"

Cerdic answered firmly: "You have received food as guests. But we have no great store. Your friends who belong to Wealdor know that in this season all must work."

The other's face darkened with rage.

"Boy. We are warriors. We do not work with the women in the fields. We guard the stockade and meet attacks. We do not follow oxen to pasture."

Guthlac raised an eyebrow and growled: "I have not seen you guard aught but beer pots."

The warrior ignored him. He strode down the table, seized a child by the arm, dragged it from the bench and drew his dagger.

"If we are not fed, I'll cut the whelp's throat."

Cerdic rose, his face pale, but Guthlac dragged him down to his seat. "We are not enough to fight six trained warriors. They will see women and children die. They have no hearts. Let the women bring them food."

This was done, and the grinning warriors settled down to eat. That night they drank and sang till dawn and then fell asleep across the table.

In the morning the friends gathered again outside the hall and talked together anxiously. Djamila, her eyes glinting with mischief, her fingers flashing, laid out a plan. Hilde approved it and went to see it carried out without delay. Later, when the sun was high, the warriors woke and staggered out into the light of day, seeking food. But the kitchen and the fire trench were deserted. Not a morsel of food, not a bowl was to be seen. They looked around, savagely seeking someone to demand food from, but no one was to be seen. The women and children were all gone.

Muttering angrily, the warriors searched the village, blundering in and out of homes, even poking inside the empty cattle pens. But they found nothing.

They drew together in a puzzled group in the doorway of the hall. Then two of them, Oswy of Wealdor and one of the strangers, were sent to the meadows in search of the women. The two men, irritated and bewildered by hunger and heads still sore from the night's drinking, set off into the woods, walking carelessly, their heads down. Faint rustlings in the small bushes were ignored. But when they saw two young women ahead of them through the trees they forgot their hunger and went in pursuit. The girls ran farther into the woods, leading the men on, stopping every now and then to look back and laugh. Now the warriors became angry again and, unbuckling their harness to give them greater freedom, they left the path and cut through the undergrowth to head off their quarry. Just when it seemed the men would lay hold of them, the girls leapt aside, shrieking with laughter. The ground collapsed beneath the warriors' pounding feet and they dropped into darkness.

Inside the stockade the four others waited. The sun was past its height and beginning to lean down towards the west. The trees outside the gate cast longer shadows. And still their companions had not come back from the woods. Ecfrith muttered to the leader: "I'll wager my brother has found the women and filled his belly while we wait here."

The leader was about to reply when, in the opening of the fence, two girls appeared, basket on arm as though bringing food. The warriors grinned and waited, but the girls came no nearer. Ecfrith yelled at them, but they did not move. He leapt up and, followed by another of the band, charged across the open space. But the girls were already well into the trees. The two warriors soon disappeared into the woods, and the last two were left alone in the deserted village.

Another hour passed in silence, but now the anger and the hunger had become sharpened by nervousness. The leader paced about before the meet-hall, loosening his sword in its scabbard. As the sun began to set, the noise of laughter and chattering came from the woods outside.

"Ecfrith was right," growled the leader. "And he has played us the same trick. Feeding himself while we go hungry." Then he stared in amazement. For through the stockade gate came a strange procession. First giggling boys and girls chasing one another and driving hens and pigs. Then came women and old men from the fields, talking and laughing. They moved at a leisurely pace through the centre of the village, past the astonished warriors, and into the meet-hall, which soon rang with the sounds of cheerful eating and drinking. With a snarl of rage, the leader drew his sword and hurled himself at the doorway. But his way was barred as if by magic. The vast figure of Guthlac, sword drawn, stood in front of him.

"Ho ho. He seeks more children to do battle with. Try your strength with this babe in arms."

And laughing at his own joke, Guthlac swung his own sword, sending the warrior's weapon flying into the fire trench five paces away. At the same moment the second warrior was seized from behind and disarmed. The two were dragged swiftly into the hall, where Cerdic and his mother sat with Stiglaf and Aelwyn at their side. Cerdic spoke in a voice tinged with contempt:

"A day's hunger has taught you little. But you shall see."

While the two warriors stood fuming and powerless, through the open door came their four companions. They were disarmed, their clothes muddy and torn. But these four went straight to the tables where places were laid for them, and before the eyes of their leader they ate greedily.

"Your companions have agreed to accept our law and custom. They shall eat. And you likewise, if you accept."

The warrior leader spat.

"I accept nothing. And those who do shall regret it."

"Then you shall leave Wealdor and not return," replied Cerdic.

The leader, his lean, dark face twisted, his eyes glittering, strode to the door, his only companion following him silently. Cerdic raised his voice: "Your weapons and harness you will find in the woods beyond the gate. Do not seek to return. And tell any who seek the way to Wealdor, they must first learn its ways."

17

A month passed without event. The people of Wealdor went about their spring sowing, though time was spared to strengthen the stockade, and care was taken that a good lookout was maintained on both landward and seaward sides of the village. But the victory over the masterless men and the fact that their going had left Wealdor four men stronger, gave the people courage, and as the days passed the excitement of the early spring was forgotten.

Stiglaf was still uneasy, however, and as he began to know his way through the forests, he spent more and more time in long marches and roamings into their depths. He kept watch on the land around and at the same time satisfied his hunger, which he had felt since his exile from the Skalling valley, for the smell of the woods in his nostrils. Each day, as he learned the secret ways, he ventured farther out, sometimes circling miles from the village. To his friends it seemed as though he were searching for and expecting something.

One morning he had reached high ground in the woods some miles from the village and paused where he had a clear view to the west. Below him the trees stretched away green and moving, like waves in the sea. And his sharp eye caught sight of other movement. Limping to the foot of a large tree, he stretched out his long arms and hauled himself into the upper branches. From there his straining eyes picked out distant horsemen. He counted them slowly and carefully. There could not be less than a score, and a shadow of danger crossed Stiglaf's mind. To him there was no doubt that the leader of the warrior band was making good his wish for revenge by bringing others to exact a price for the insult he had suffered.

Easing himself down the trunk of the tree, Stiglaf circled the track on which the horsemen rode and came up on them unseen.

He picked his way well and found a vantage point some little way ahead, where from a tree branch he could watch the path more closely. It was not long before he heard the clink of horse's harness and then the first horseman came in sight – a splendidly armed warrior. By his side rode an unarmed man, short and squat but richly dressed and bearing himself arrogantly. Stiglaf peered and it seemed to him like a dream or vision. For the warrior who rode at the head of the column was unmistakable – that lean, dark and cruel face, with its thin lips. This was the man he had seen one day in the woods above the valley of the Skallings in the year before his father had sailed away to his death. The horseman was Cynewulf, who had been Harald Fine-hair's captain, Cynewulf who had lured the Skalling men away to war, Cynewulf the exile who had managed to return to his own land.

He recalled the words of Hilde, of the lord who had taken the young men of Wealdor into his fighting force – "the cruellest face I ever saw". Without a doubt this was the same man, plying the same evil trade in his own land that he plied in exile in the land of the Northmen. And that opulent, proud man at his side must be the abbot of whom Cerdic's mother spoke so bitterly.

Stiglaf waited no longer but slithered rapidly down the tree and set off in the awkward shambling run he had practised so well, using all the shortest ways through the woods to make good time back to the village. As he reached the meadows he met Cerdic, Aelwyn and Djamila walking quietly together. He took Cerdic on one side and swiftly described what he had seen.

"We must get the women and children into hiding," said Cerdic.

Stiglaf shook his head. "There is not time. The horsemen would cross their path as they went to the safe entrance. What is more, Cerdic, I believe this is no simple raiding party.

"These are men seeking a parley. Else why is the abbot with them?"

"That man of God would join a raiding party if it suited him."

"True, but we have no choice. They will try to outface us. We must outwit them. Come," said Stiglaf, "here is what we must do."

An hour later a horn sounded outside the stockade and a warrior stood in the gate.

"Earl Cynewulf and Bishop Gregory would talk with the men of Wealdor."

The answer came: "Let them enter with an escort of two. Let the other men wait beyond the fence."

The gate swung wide and the earl and the man of God entered on foot, attended by two warriors. Once inside they halted. The great seat of Cerdic the founder of Wealdor was drawn out in the open before the meet-hall doorway.

On it sat Hilde, straight, white-haired and proud, and by her side Cerdic in a rich blue cloak, holding the ancient sword of Wealdor's chiefs. Around them, fully harnessed, were Guthlac, Oswy and Ecfrith, and before them stood Aelwyn, brown robed. In the shadow of the doorway were grouped more figures leaning on spears. Cynewulf took in this unexpected sight, shrewdly weighing up numbers and arms, and then smiled:

"Greetings, young lord. Your face I do not know."

"But we know yours, Earl Cynewulf, and yours too, Abbot Gregory, who now flies high as bishop," retorted Hilde austerely. "You are not welcome here and you know it. My husband Brydo, the father of Cerdic here, and two-score and more of our young men are dead and yours is the blame."

"You speak harshly," the bishop replied smoothly. "But my heart rejoices to see your son grown so tall and straight and wear the cloak of his fathers so seemly. And my heart rejoices yet more to see that a brother of our faith is part of your household." He nodded to Aelwyn, raised his voice and went on:

"The word of God spreads over the land despite all that heathen princes and tyrants do to halt it. The word of God is like a many-branched tree spreading over the world."

Aelwyn stepped forward, his eyes unseeing, yet facing the bishop unerringly.

"In the shade of your tree no grass grows and in its twigs no bird sings. Its branches hang men and its roots drink blood. Your god is not my god, nor the god of the people of Wealdor."

There came a murmur of approval from the dark figures

in the doorway. The bishop opened his mouth to reply furiously, but Cynewulf forestalled him.

"Cerdic, son of Brydo, we did not come to discuss matters of faith for they are not in our understanding. We came rather to discuss law and custom, which I am told have great weight in Wealdor."

"Say what you need, Earl Cynewulf, and do not hold us here," answered Cerdic. "My mother has told you that you are not welcome, and you must respect her word."

"I will waste no words. Wealdor harbours four men who are of my band and have eaten my bread and have gone away from me."

"Two of these men, Ecfrith and Oswy, are not of your band and went with you freely to fight, but returned of their own free will and remain here. The other two have taken refuge with us and we have given them shelter. If they have committed crimes, Wealdor takes those harms on itself and if it be possible will make recompense to those who have suffered wrong. But I know of no crimes these men have done. They have killed only in battle."

Cynewulf's smile faded.

"I know of old customs. And I know the law of the kingdom, which says that each man shall have his lord, and setting aside the men of Wealdor, these two are my men."

"I know naught of such law. The law of refuge is my guide, as it guided my fathers before me."

"Aye," retorted Cynewulf. "And Wealdor has become a haven for every wandering rogue in the kingdom, like that fat scoundrel who stands behind you, a murderer in his own village. And they tell me that Wealdor even gives refuge to Northmen exiled from their own lands for unspeakable crimes and harbouring of witches."

Stiglaf stepped forward from the shadow of the meet-hall doorway. "But for the law of refuge, Earl Cynewulf, you would be a dead man to-day."

"Who is this cripple?" demanded Cynewulf.

"I am Stiglaf, son of Sven Fork-beard, chief of the Skallings, a man whom you knew when you were in exile in the house of Harald Fine-hair, where no man demanded of you an account of your past and no one drove you away."

Cynewulf's lips curved in a slow smile: "Why, yes, we are known to one another. Your cousin Torald was a battle-comrade of mine and I am sworn to do him service if I can. He would count it a service if I told him where his arm could stretch to pluck out of hiding the one he hates most, next to the black witch who killed his father."

At the venom of these words, Stiglaf unthinkingly looked round to where Djamila had been standing in the hall. But the dark girl had vanished.

Cerdic stepped forward. "There shall be no venting of old quarrels inside these walls. Our answer is given. Unless it can be shown beyond doubt that these two warriors have done deeds that no man may forgive, they shall not be forced to leave."

Cynewulf laughed: "I came to treat reasonably with you, though I have force enough to take these men, whether you willed it or not. But you have chosen to use strong words when you have not the means to back them. I will have my way by the oldest law of all, the right of might. I will give you a space to think again. We shall wait outside your fence and you shall send the two men out to us. If not, then we shall enter again and take away as hostage whom we will, warriors or women."

Cynewulf turned on his heel and, followed by the bishop, strode away to the gate. But he had gone no more than half a dozen paces when one of his men ran to meet him with a cry of alarm.

"Lord, we are in danger. There are armed men in the woods on all sides."

"Armed men? There can be no armed men. Unless they played us false about their numbers. But that cannot be."

"But it is true, lord. We are out-numbered two to one. They wait for us among the trees, with bows and spears."

Baffled, but seizing his chance, Cerdic stepped forward.

"Take your chance and be gone, Earl Cynewulf. Take your men from our land while you may and do not return."

Raging, Cynewulf strode to the gate and swung on to his horse. The bishop was already mounted and ready to go, looking nervously round him. As they rode away, surrounded by their men, Cynewulf jerked the head of his mount and raised his fist.

"I will repay this insult two-fold and in a way that will strike home."

And with that they were away, galloping down the forest track.

Cerdic and his friends were left staring after them, open-mouthed with surprise. Aelwyn raised his hands to the sky.

"A miracle. Deliverance from the sky," he cried.

"Hm," muttered Guthlac. "It smacks more of witchcraft to me." And as he spoke, from the gate there came a soft chuckle, as round the gate-post peered a helmeted head followed by another and another.

"Goblins," cried Guthlac, as a shriek of laughter came from beyond the stockade and through the gate rushed a score of strange figures, harnessed and helmeted and waving swords, bows and spears. Stiglaf was first to recognise the leader of the miraculous armed band and burst into laughter himself.

"Why, the men of Wealdor were saved by the women," he shouted, and the whole village resounded with laughter as the armed girls, led by Djamila, marched up to the great seat before the meet-hall. Guthlac roared louder than the rest. "Why, Earl Cynewulf and his warriors were foxed by a bunch of girls playing in the woods with harness their fathers and brothers left behind."

"Not playing," Hilde rebuked him. "They were in earnest. And you'll agree, in the dark of the woods, they can work as well on the fears of guilty men as true warriors can." She turned to Djamila and placed an arm round her shoulders.

"It was a happy day that brought you to our shores, dark princess, and your fair brother from the north, and you, good Guthlac. With your aid, we do not need an army."

Aelwyn ran for his harp and while the people crowded round, he swiftly made a new song:

"The man of God, whom God could never know,
A high-born lord who could not stoop too low.
Two-score bold men whose courage swift did go,
Young women's wiles did quickly overthrow."

Spring wore away into summer, the hottest summer Wealdor had known for many years. The hay shone yellow in the meadows and was quickly gathered in. Deep in the woods, brush and trees burst into flame and smoke curled on the skyline. As June and July passed, it began to seem that the crops would be burned up too in the terrible heat of the sun. During the day people sheltered in their homes, going out to work only in the cool of the evening, while dogs and children wandered listlessly around, scratching in the dry dust. The sea, calm as a lake, stretched away to the misty horizon, and man and beast waited for rain.

In the evening, after work, when the sun dipped over the woods, the four friends would often gather to sit on the short brown turf of the cliffs to talk of their travels. And sometimes Cerdic and his mother would join them, and the talk would turn to more serious matters.

"If we can live in peace and safety for another five years, then all will be well," said Hilde one evening. "In that time many of our boys will be grown and we shall count a full score of warriors."

"That is, if we count our good friends," said Cerdic. "Surely we cannot ask them to stay and fight our battles for ever."

Guthlac chewed on a short blade of grass. "I for one would ask nothing better than to live out my life in Wealdor, my second home. And if I should end my days in harness, fighting on the stockade, then that would be all one to me. When a man finds true friends he is in no haste to go away again."

"And what of Stiglaf and Djamila?" asked Hilde.

Djamila laid her fingers on Hilde's hand and did no more.

Stiglaf said: "I often long for a sight of my own people, even of those who cast me out. And I have promised Djamila that one day I shall help her find a way home to her family. But those are things for other days. Now Wealdor is our home and we shall always be ready to help its folk when they are in need."

"And we shall always be ready to come to your aid if need be," answered Cerdic.

"How can we be in danger here, save from your foes?" asked Stiglaf, smiling.

"Who can know what the future will bring?" said Hilde, as she rose and walked slowly back to the village, followed by the others.

Days passed in golden heat and then, in August, the evenings brought dark purple clouds that gathered on the horizon. But each morning these clouds vanished, leaving the sky clear again. At night, as darkness fell, lightning flickered on the line between sea and sky, and thunder rumbled in the distance. But still no rain fell and the heat remained oppressive. Day by day the deep angry cloudbank on the eastern skyline began to grow. The air was full of the menace of a coming storm, and the people went about their tasks uneasily, unwillingly, as if fearing to be caught unprepared. Eyes constantly strayed towards the sea, where the clouds now stood thick and heavy, shot through now and then by lightning. One evening, as the friends stood on the cliffs watching the play of lightning on the horizon, Djamila grasped Stiglaf's arm and urgently made a sign on his palm.

"Ships."

But Stiglaf shook his head. He could see nothing.

When the morning came, though, a lookout from the clifftop came running to where people gathered for the day's first meal. He stumbled as he ran, and gasped:

"Ships at sea. Two sails. One red, one black."

18

The lookout's message shocked the Wealdor people into silence as they gathered in a great crowd before the meet-hall. Cerdic mounted swiftly on the stump of a tree that stood near the doorway.

"Good people. Have no fear. We are ready for attack. We will meet them on the cliffs and crush them with boulders as they try to climb. They will never reach the stockade, let alone storm the meet-hall."

"No, Cerdic. This is madness," cried Stiglaf. "I know what those two sails, one red, one black, can mean. You do not. Four-score men ride in those two ships, four-score fighting men used to the sea and mountains, Skalling men, fierce raiders. They will swarm up your cliffs like the sea-birds fly. You are not strong enough to resist them and many will die needlessly."

"Die needlessly? What does that mean?" demanded Cerdic.

Stiglaf answered firmly:

"Those ships come on one quest, and one only. My cousin Torald, chief of the Skallings since his father died, will have his revenge on me and on Djamila here because he hates us and chooses to believe that she caused his father's death. As long as I live he will never feel safe as

Skalling chief. He calls me Stiglaf the cripple. I am his kin, but he fears and hates me."

"Then if he be your foe, though he is your kin, then he is our foe," said Cedric. "He shall not lay a hand on you, nor the dark maid, while we draw breath." And the handful of warriors in the crowd shouted their agreement. But Stiglaf shook his head.

"It may not be. I will not have it, Cerdic. You must do as I say. Your duty is to shelter your people, your women and your children. You dare not put their lives in peril for the sake of our friendship."

Stiglaf turned to the crowd.

"Hear me, people of Wealdor. The two ships bear my cousin Torald and his men. Their quarrel is only with me. You must go into your safe hiding in the cliff and I will wait on the shore for the ships to come. My cousin hates me, but he is no fool. He will not risk the lives of his warriors to have me by fighting if he can have me without striking a blow. I give you my word that if you do as I say, by the time the sun is down, the raiders' ships will be below the skyline and Wealdor will be safe from them again."

"Nay, Stiglaf. I will not have it. You are our kin," said Cerdic. But his mother, tears in her eyes, intervened.

"Stiglaf is right. He has his fate to face. You have yours, Cerdic. It is hard for you to see. But Stiglaf understands what is right, just as his mother Deira did before him. The lives of the helpless shall not be cast away in the name of friendship." She stepped up to Stiglaf and embraced him warmly. "You are a true son, not only of your father, great Sven Fork-beard, but a true son of your mother, Deira, who held the lives of others more highly than her own. Come," she called to the other women. "Make all ready, we must drive the cattle down into the caves before the ships come close to land. You know what has to be done."

Sadly the women and old men obeyed her, with many backward glances at Stiglaf. At Cerdic's command the small band of warriors went with them, then Cerdic, regretfully and shaking his head, clasped Stiglaf's shoulders in his arms and bid him farewell.

"We shall never forget what you do to-day, Stiglaf," he whispered.

Hilde put her arm around Djamila and said: "Come, child. We shall take care of you."

But Djamila shook aside the arm and with quick steps gripped hold of Stiglaf's hand.

Her fingers gestured her refusal, and on Stiglaf's wrist she made the sign: "I stay with you. You cannot send me away."

Stiglaf attempted to free his hand from hers, but the dark fingers had unbelievable strength. He could not break loose without injuring her. Then Guthlac stepped up.

"I claim the right, as your travel companion, to be with you to the end. The Wealdor folk may shift without me."

"I, too," called Aelwyn, stumbling forward, his arms stretched out to find Stiglaf. "We four journeyed together. We shall not be parted."

Stiglaf looked at the village, now fast emptying of people as the Wealdor folk, driving their cattle before them, streamed towards the safety of the caverns. He recalled the day, almost a year before, when he had first seen it, emptied as to-day, by the threat of a dragon-prowed ship. It had been a good home and he had found good friends. But his journeying must begin again. Not that this next journey would last long. Torald would make sure it came swiftly to an end. He turned resolutely to Guthlac and Aelwyn.

"If you be my true friends, then you shall do my will. I command you to go with the people of Wealdor who have need of you. Where I go my dearest friends cannot follow."

Sadly Aelwyn turned away. Guthlac hesitated, then reached out for Djamila's arm to drag her away. But her eyes flashed to him with such fury that he shook his heavy grey head hopelessly and went without a word in the wake of the last of the Wealdor folk, while Stiglaf, with Djamila clinging to his arm, walked slowly towards the cliff path.

As they made their way down the narrow cleft in the chalk to the beach they saw the first dragon prow push into the harbour.

As they reached the beach, the red-sailed craft was leading the way, while the black-sailed craft hung back. Stiglaf knew then that he was right. There would be no general landing or raid. Uncertain of the forces awaiting them, Torald and his men would be content to snatch their prize and sail away.

Stiglaf and Djamila sat down on a large rock some little distance from the water's edge and waited while the red-sailed ship, pushed forward by great sweeps of the oars, came steadily towards them. By force of habit, Stiglaf counted the oars. There were only thirty. Had Torald's crew suffered losses in some raid or battle? No matter. Thirty men would be enough to seize one cripple and a dumb girl. He smiled to himself as the dragon prow surged on. Above the bay the purple clouds filled the sky. The air was stifling. The storm must come soon, thought Stiglaf And as the thought left his mind, a jagged flash of lightning cut through the purple to the east, and a tearing roll of thunder sounded from the heart of the clouds. Then in the quiet that followed came Torald's voice as, from his look-out point on the prow, he caught sight of the two figures seated on the rock.

"Ho, Stiglaf the cripple. Meet your fate. You and the witch. I have sailed from the Skalling Valley, straight as a spear, to find you."

The red-sailed ship ran ashore, the prow biting deeply nto the sand. The crew backed their oars. A great flash of lightning and explosion of thunder shook the bay as Torald, fully armed and harnessed, leapt into the shallows.

"Ho, Stiglaf the cripple. I cannot kill a man like a sheep. Take this."

Torald, thigh-deep in water now rippling with the first drops of rain, raised his arm. Something flashed in the light as it curved through the air. A sword fell point first, at Stiglaf's feet and buried itself half-way to the hilt in the sand.

"Ho, Stiglaf. Are you man enough to fight? Meet me in open fight and if you win, the witch shall live. If you die, she dies too. Take the sword and fight. I know you have sworn never to spill blood. Now you must choose. Break your oath or I will kill the witch before your eyes."

Stiglaf placed himself in front of Djamila. His hand slowly lowered itself to the sword hilt as though by its own will. It was foolish. He had never laid hands on a sword before. Yet he was amazed to feel the blood suddenly rush through his veins like fire. Gripping the hilt with both hands, he whirled the blade round his head.

"Come on, Torald. Now our fates meet. We both know what my fate is. But what did Unna, the wise woman, prophesy for you?" He stepped forward, swinging the sword as a thunderous roll shook the very ground Torald and he stood on.

"She foretold that I should rule the Skallings," shouted Torald. And again came the sound of thunder and the tremor from the ground.

"And what else, Torald? What else? Did she foretell nothing beyond? You are ruler of the Skallings. Did she foretell your end?" Stiglaf stood his ground, gripping the sword hilt and waiting for Torald's attack.

Torald stood stock still, his feet astride, ten paces from Stiglaf and ten paces from the sea. But he advanced no farther. He seemed gripped by some strange force that would not let him stir. His eyes were fixed beyond Stiglaf's shoulder as from the cliff came yet another tremor and thunderous noise. But Stiglaf knew suddenly that this was not thunder. Still facing Torald, he turned his eye. Behind him, the curtain of bushes and trees that masked the cliff-face opened and, with roaring bellows of terror and pain, one after another the huge, long-horned Wealdor cattle burst from the face of the rock. Crazed by the lightning and thunder, and the pelting rain, the cattle stampeded down the beach. They bunched together, butted and leapt on one another. At the rock where Djamila sat they parted and crashed by on either side. In front of them Torald, his red-bearded features frozen in terror, crouched as if trying to draw himself together. Then with a gigantic effort he broke free from the spell and turned to run as two-score fear-maddened cattle thundered down on him.

"Torald! Throw yourself down!" shouted Stiglaf.

But Torald heard nothing. The horns of a great steer took him in the back and his body leapt into the air as if it were

a bundle of rags. Down it fell, only to rise in the air again as if it were thistledown. Then the cattle were past him, over him, racing into the sea, while the thunder drummed over the passing of Torald, son of Red Arnulf, whose body lay broken and torn a few paces from the water's edge. Stiglaf raced to Torald and dropped on one knee beside him. His cousin's chest still rose and fell feebly. The cheek muscles above the red beard twitched as Torald tried to speak. Stiglaf bent down his head until his cousin's lips were close and he heard the faint whisper.

"I did not tell you all, Stiglaf. Unna the old woman of

the hills foretold that at my death I would be lower than the lowest. It has come about."

Torald's twitching lips were still.

His head sank back on the sand. Stiglaf rose and, looking across the water to the red-sailed ship, he called out:

"Skallings, hear me. Torald, my cousin and your chief, is dead. I did not seek his death, though he sought mine. Our quarrel is at an end."

At the prow of the longship appeared a young warrior, one of Torald's closest followers. His face was livid with grief and rage, and he cried out:

"Now we shall land and make an end of you, Stiglaf the Unsteady, cause of all our trouble. Make ready to meet death."

Amid the roar of thunder, the lightning and the rain, came a deeper sound from the cliff-face behind Stiglaf. Again the screen of bushes was pushed aside and more cattle and beasts of all sizes began to push their way through, while behind them in the cliff came the sound of singing and shouting. The warrior at the prow of the longship fell silent in amazement. The cattle of Wealdor poured out from the opening and filled the beach, milling around the rock where Djamila sat, pressing round the space of sand where Stiglaf stood next to his cousin's body. And behind the beasts, singing to the music of Aelwyn's harp, came the people of Wealdor, warriors and old men, women and children. Their song swelled out between bursts of thunder, which now began slowly to die away, while the rain washed down and in the east came the first streak of blue sky under the storm clouds. The gigantic voice of Guthlac boomed out over the bay.

"Northmen, hear me. If you will kill Stiglaf, our true friend, you must slaughter us all, every one, man, woman, child and beast of the field, for we all stand between you and him."

Unseen hands pulled down the young Skalling warrior from the prow of the red-sailed ship and in his place appeared a strange figure, gaunt and white-haired.

With a shock Stiglaf recognised Eynor, his father's old comrade. "Stiglaf. Eynor, friend of your father, speaks. Heed not the word of a young hothead and fool. The death of Torald heals all wounds. We do not seek to harm your friends."

Supported by two young men, the old warrior climbed from the ship and with halting step moved through the shallows to the shore. Stiglaf ran forward, pushing through the milling cattle, to Eynor's side, and the two embraced. Stiglaf stared at the old warrior.

"Things have gone badly with you, Eynor, since I last saw you."

"Things have gone ill for the Skalling people since you were driven from our valley," replied Eynor, and as he spoke, the Wealdor folk moved closer, crowding round, while the warriors of either side eyed one another curiously and cautiously. Eynor continued, his voice tired and weak.

"You thought, maybe, that four-score men rode in our ships?" He laughed bitterly. "Stiglaf, these two ships hold all that is left of the Skalling people. The ship of Red Arnulf, at the command of Torald, was manned by everyone, boy, warrior or greybeard who could pull on an oar. The other ship holds women, children and some cattle. Thus Torald thought to deceive you and have his revenge. Your friends here need have no fear. The Skalling people have not the strength nor the will to attack others. For the last four days our people have barely eaten."

Cerdic and Hilde pushed their way forward through the crowd of beasts and men.

"Are there women and children in your ships and starving?" asked Hilde, amazed.

"It is so," replied Eynor. "I fear that many will die if they do not eat soon."

"Then that must not happen," she replied. "Let your ships be drawn up on to the beach. Our people will drive back the beasts to their places and go back to our village to make ready for your coming. Then, when your ships are made fast against more storms, Stiglaf and my son Cerdic shall bring your folk to the hall. They shall eat and drink of the best that we have."

"You have great mercy on those who attacked you," said Eynor.

"Your leader Sven Fork-beard had more than mercy for my kinswoman Deira. There is no quarrel between us. Come, old man, you shall sit at our table to-night."

Night was close at hand by the time the last of the Skallings, in all thirty men and boys and little more than a score women and girls, some sick and all weak from hunger, had been helped up the cliff and into the village. The cattle were driven back through the cave and out into the woods, and as the sun set, the meet-hall filled with young and old, both Skalling and Wealdor folk. The children were cared for and put to rest, and the two peoples sat together and ate.

For Stiglaf it was hard to see the faces he knew well so shrunken and pale and to know that this was all that still lived of a once proud people. When all had done with eating, he turned to Eynor and bade him speak, to tell the whole story of the Skallings. Eynor began, and when his voice faltered the tale was taken up by others.

"It was foretold to Arnulf that his son Torald should rule the Skallings, and so it was. But it was also foretold, and none but Torald and Arnulf knew this, that Torald would take death to the southern sea and bring it back. And this he did. When you left the valley, Stiglaf, Torald took with him the young men and sailed south. But so many fell in battle that barely enough remained to bring the longships home. And there was worse to come.

"Many of those who returned bore with them a strange sickness from the south which raged through the valley, killing like a mad raider.

"But, when we believed we had felt the worst blow of fate, we felt yet another. In the winter the people of the hill came down and asked that in return for past help, the pledge of Stiglaf should be honoured, and they be allowed to graze their herds in the valley. Torald, for no good reason but his hatred for Stiglaf, denied them this, and seized one of their maidens as hostage until they left the valley. But instead of leaving, the hill people brought down their beasts in hundreds and drove them through the valley, destroying everything before them, shelter for cattle and men. The Skallings were forced to flee aboard their ships, and Torald had to set free the hostage. But it was all too late and the homesteads were destroyed. We had to sail to the south seeking refuge.

"But this still did not calm Torald's rage. From the south he had word from one of Harald Fine-hair's men that Stiglaf and the dark maid had taken refuge in the western islands, in the place from where Sven Fork-beard had taken his wife. And so this last mad voyage was attempted, chancing all the fortunes of the Skallings for revenge. And so the last prophecy of Unna of the Hills was fulfilled, and Torald at his death was lower than the lowest."

In the deep silence that followed Eynor's story, Cerdic rose and said:

"Skalling people. I have spoken with my people. As you shall hear, we have suffered losses too, for men's greed and hate. We have space at our hearths and room at our tables, empty homes, husbandless wives and fatherless children, as you have. In the days gone by, Wealdor took in men and women from across the sea. Let it be so again. It will be if you will join with us."

For a while no Skalling answered, then Eynor spoke up.

"Let Stiglaf, son of Sven, speak for us," and the others agreed.

"Let it be so," answered Stiglaf. "One day there may be Skallings who will seek to return to their valley. Let the longships lie in harbour against that time and let Skalling live with Wealdor folk, like teeth in a comb.

"Do not look to me as leader, but to Cerdic. For I will still go on my wanderings. I must take Djamila back to her family's home. Our little ship still lies down by the shore ready to sail, and if there are friends who will ride with us, when the time is ripe, they will be thrice welcome.

"But now," cried Stiglaf, "Aelwyn, take your harp and sing."

And Aelwyn struck his harp and sang:

"*What has no eyes but sees all that passes?*
What hears no evil but knows good?
What has no tongue but says all that is needful?
What cannot run, but is everywhere?"

And from round the hall came the answer.

"*Friendship, the love of true friends.*"